WEB PROGRAMMING
WITH PHP AND MYSQL

CODE AND CONNECT

RAMA SUBBANNA S
RAJINI M

notionpress
.com

INDIA · SINGAPORE · MALAYSIA

Dedicated to

Our beloved children, Rachel and Rayna
– Dr. Rama Subbanna S, Rajini M

CONTENTS

FOREWORD

It is with great pleasure that I present this book, **Code and Connect: Web Programming Using PHP and SQL**, written by Dr. S. Rama Subbanna to the academic community. In an era where web technologies are revolutionizing the world, this comprehensive guide is tailored to meet the needs of students across all branches.

The book provides a structured approach to mastering the fundamentals of web programming, seamlessly integrating PHP and SQL to build robust and dynamic web applications. Through its well-illustrated examples, hands-on exercises, and practical insights, students will find themselves equipped with the skills essential for both academic success and professional growth in the tech-driven world.

One of the highlights of this book is its accessibility. The concepts are presented in a manner that is both engaging and easy to understand, making it an invaluable resource for beginners and advanced learners alike. Additionally, the emphasis on practical applications ensures that students can immediately see the relevance of what they are learning in real-world scenarios.

I am confident that this book will serve as a stepping stone for engineering students to explore the vast opportunities in web development and beyond. It stands as a testament to the authors' dedication to education and their passion for empowering the next generation of engineers.

I congratulate the author Dr. Rama Subbanna on this remarkable achievement and wish the readers a fruitful learning journey.

Dr. Y. Rajasree Rao
Principal,
ISTS Women's Engineering College,
Rajahmundry,
Andhra Pradesh, India

PREFACE

In the ever-evolving landscape of web development, PHP stands as a stalwart, powering millions of websites and applications worldwide. As a server-side scripting language, PHP's primary strength lies in its ability to seamlessly integrate with HTML and interact with databases, making it an indispensable tool for creating dynamic web content.

This book delves into the foundational elements that make PHP a vital part of any developer's toolkit. From understanding syntax and data types to exploring advanced concepts such as object-oriented programming and error handling, we will uncover the essential components that enable you to harness the full power of PHP.

As we embark on this journey, we will not only cover the core features of PHP but also examine best practices and modern techniques that enhance code efficiency and maintainability. Whether you are a novice eager to learn or an experienced programmer looking to refine your skills, this book aims to provide a comprehensive guide to mastering PHP.

Join us as we build a solid framework for understanding PHP, laying the groundwork for creating robust web applications that can meet the demands of today's digital landscape. Together, we will unlock the potential of this versatile language and empower you to bring your web development ideas to life.

THE BUILDING BLOCKS OF PHP

Introduction:

PHP stands for **"PHP: Hypertext Preprocessor"**. It was created by Danish-Canadian programmer Rasmus Lerdorf in 1993 and officially released to the public in 1995. PHP is a widely used server-side scripting language designed for creating dynamic web pages. It is open-source, meaning it is free to download and use.

PHP is known for its simplicity and ease of learning. The fundamental components required to write PHP programs are often referred to as the "building blocks" of PHP. Here are some of the basic building blocks of PHP.

1.1 Creating a Simple PHP Program:

A PHP script starts with <? php and ends with ?>

The default file extension for PHP files is ".php".

Syntax:

```
<?php
// PHP Code
?>
```

1.1.1 Rules for Executing a PHP Program in a Browser:

A web browser and a PHP web server are needed to run a PHP program.

- Write the code in a text editor (such as Notepad).

- Save the file with any name followed by the .php extension.

- If XAMPP is installed on the C: drive, save the file in C:\xampp\htdocs\ yourfolder.

- Open the file in a browser using the URL http://localhost/yourfolder/ filename.php

1.1.2   Rules for Executing a PHP Program in the Command Prompt:

- **Open Terminal or Command Prompt:**

  Open Command Prompt or PowerShell by searching for it in the Start menu.

- **Navigate to the Directory Containing PHP Files:**

  Use the cd command (which stands for "change directory") to navigate to the folder where PHP files are located.

- **Run PHP Code:**

  Execute the PHP file using the **php** command followed by the filename. php.

Syntax:

```
php filename.php
```

1.2   Variables:

A variable is a container that stores data values.

1.2.1   Rules for Declaring Variables:

A variable starts with the $ sign followed by the name of the variable.

- A variable name must start with a letter or an underscore.

- A variable name cannot start with a number.

- A variable name can only contain alphanumeric characters and underscores.

- Variable names are case-sensitive.

- No whitespace is allowed within the variable name.

- A variable name must not be a reserved word or keyword.

Examples:

$a, $b1, and $v_r are valid variable names.

1.3   Browser Output:

In PHP, there are two ways to produce output to the browser:

1.3.1   echo Statement:

The **echo** statement is used to output one or more strings. It is one of the most commonly used methods for displaying content. The echo statement can be used with or without parentheses: echo or echo().

Program 1.3.1(a): Printing a String Using the echo Statement:

```php
<?php
 echo "Hello world";
 ?>
```

Program 1.3.1(b): Printing a Variable's Value Using the echo Statement:

```php
<?php
 $a=5;
echo $a;
 ?>
```

1.3.2   print statement:

The print statement is similar to echo but with slightly different behavior. It always returns 1, which allows it to be used in expressions. The print statement can serve as an alternative to echo and is also a language construct, so it can be used with or without parentheses (i.e., print or print()).

Program 1.3.2: Printing a String Value Using the print Statement:

```php
<?php
$result = print("Hello, World!");
print $result;
 ?>
```

In the above example, print returns a value of 1, whereas echo does not return anything.

1.3.3 Differences Between echo and print Statements in PHP

Factor	echo statement	print statement
Arguments	Accepts a list of arguments (multiple arguments can be passed), separated by commas.	Accepts only one argument at a time.
Return Value	Does not return any value.	Returns the value 1.
Performance	Faster.	Slower .
Recommendation	More commonly recommended for its flexibility and performance.	Less commonly recommended, primarily due to its return value and slight performance difference.

1.4 Reading User Input with readline( ) in PHP:

The **readline( )** function is a built-in function in PHP used to read a line of input from the command line interface. It allows the user to input data that can be processed by the PHP script.

Program 1.4.1: Reading a String with readline( ) in PHP:

```php
<?php
// Read a string input from the user
$input = readline("Enter a string: ");
echo " String is: " . $input;
?>
```

In this program, the readline() function is used to read a string input from the user. The **readline( )** function captures input from the command line as a string. After the user enters the string, it is stored in the $input variable, and echo is used to display the entered string.

Steps to Run a PHP Program from the Command Line:

To execute a PHP program from the command prompt (CLI), follow these steps:

1. Open the **Command Prompt** (on Windows) or **Terminal** (on macOS/ Linux).

2. Navigate to the directory where the PHP file is saved. For example, if the PHP file is located in a subdirectory myfolder under xampp/htdocs, use the cd command to change to that directory.

3. Run the program using the php command.

```
cd xampp/htdocs/myfolder
php stringexample.php
```

Program 1.4.2: Reading an integer value with readline( ) in PHP

```php
<?php
// Read an integer input from the user
 $a = (int) readline("Enter a number: ");
 echo "The number is: " . $a;
?>
```

In this example, the readline() function captures the input as a string. To treat the input as an integer, we use **typecasting** (int) to convert the string input into an integer. This allows you to use the input for arithmetic or other integer-related operations

The **readline()** function in PHP is designed to be used in command-line interface (CLI) environments, not in web browser environments.

1.5   Data types in PHP

In PHP, data types define the kind of data that can be stored in a variable. PHP categorizes data types into three main types: **scalar types, compound types,** and **special types**.

1.5.1   Scalar Types:

Scalar types are data types that can hold only a single value at a time. PHP's scalar types include:

1. Boolean
2. Integer
3. Float
4. String

Boolean:

A **Boolean** is a scalar data type that represents one of two possible values: true or false. Booleans are commonly used in conditional statements and logical operations.

Examples:

```
$flag1 = true;    // Represents the Boolean value true
$flag2 = false;   // Represents the Boolean value false
```

Integer:

An **integer** is a whole number without a decimal point. It can be positive, negative, or zero.

Examples:

- Positive integers: 1, 42, 999
- Negative integers: -1, -42, -999
- Zero: 0

Float: A float(or floating-point number) is a numeric data type used to represents numbers that have a decimal point or are written in scientific notation (using an exponent).

Examples:

- Decimal numbers: 3.14, -0.001, 2.718
- Scientific notation: 1.23e4 (which equals 12300), -5.67E-2 (which equals -0.0567)

String: A string is a sequence of characters enclosed in quotes. In PHP, strings can be enclosed in either single quotes (') or double quotes ("), The choice of quotes affects how the string is interpreted.
- **Single Quotes ('):** Use single quotes when you need static text and don't need variable substitution or special characters (such as escape sequences) to be interpreted inside the string.
- **Double Quotes ("):** Use double quotes when you need to include variables or interpret escape sequences like \n, \t, etc., within the string.

Program 1.5.1: Demonstrating Scalar Types in PHP

```php
<?php
$integerValue = 42;
echo "Integer Value: $integerValue\n";
$floatValue = 3.14;
echo "Float Value: $floatValue\n";
$stringValue = "Hello, World!";
echo "String Value: $stringValue\n";
$booleanValue = true;
echo "Boolean Value: " . ($booleanValue ? 'true': 'false') . "\n";
?>
```

1.5.2   Compound Types:

Compound types are data types that can hold multiple values. In PHP, there are two compound data types:

1. **Array**

2. **Object**

Array:

An **array** is a compound data type that can store multiple values in a single variable. The values stored in an array can be of different data types (e.g., integers, strings, booleans, etc.). In PHP, arrays are created using the array() function or the shorthand array syntax [].

Syntax:

```php
// Creating an array using the array() function
$numbers = array(1, 2, 3, 4, 5);
(Or)
// Creating an array using shorthand syntax
. $numbers = [5, 6, 7];
```

Object:

An object is an instance of a class that has both data (attributes or properties) and functions (methods) associated with it. Objects represent real-world entities and can be modeled to have specific characteristics (attributes) and behaviors (methods).

Examples: Real-world items like a **chair, bike, marker, pen, table, car**, and others can be represented in programming as objects. Each of these objects would have attributes (such as color, size, or speed) and methods (such as moving, writing, or turning).

1.5.3   Special Types

Special types are data types in PHP that have unique characteristics.

- **Resource:** A special data type used to reference external resources such as database connections, file handles, or network connections. Resources are typically created and managed by PHP functions or extensions.

- NULL: Null is a special data type that has only one possible value: NULL. It represents the absence of a value. If a variable is declared without being assigned a value, it is automatically assigned the value NULL.

1.6   Operators and Expressions

1.6.1   Operators:

An operator is a symbol used to perform operations on operands (values or variables). In PHP, operators are categorized into various types based on the kind of operation they perform.

Arithmetic Operators

Arithmetic operators are used to perform mathematical operations such as addition, subtraction, multiplication, and division. Below is a list of arithmetic operators along with their syntax and operations in PHP:

Operator	Name	Example	Operation
+	Addition	$a+$b	Sum of $a and $b
-	Subtraction	$a-$b	Difference of $a and $b
*	Multiplication	$a*$b	Product of $a and $b
/	Division	$a/$b	Quotient of $a and $b
%	Modulus	$a%$b	Remainder of $a divided by $b
**	Exponentiation	$a**$b	$a raised to the power of $b

Program 1.6.1: Arithmetic Operations in PHP

```php
<?php
// Get input from the user and cast it to integers
$a = (int)readline('Enter the first number: ');
$b = (int)readline('Enter the second number: ');
// Perform arithmetic operations
$addition = $a + $b;
$subtraction = $a - $b;
$multiplication = $a * $b;
$division = $b != 0 ? $a / $b: 'Division by zero error'; // Check
for division by zero
$remainder = $b != 0 ? $a % $b: 'Division by zero error'; // Check
for modulus by zero
echo "\nThe addition of $a and $b is: $addition";
echo "\nThe subtraction of $a and $b is: $subtraction";
echo "\nThe multiplication of $a and $b is: $multiplication";
echo "\nThe division of $a by $b is: $division";
echo "\nThe remainder of $a divided by $b is: $remainder";
?>
```

Logical Operators

Logical operators are used to evaluate Boolean expressions and determine their truth value. They operate on Boolean values(true or false) to combine or invert results, ultimately producing a final Boolean outcome.

Operator	Name	Example	Operation
&&	AND	$a&&$b or $a and $b	Returns TRUE if both $a and $b are true.
||	OR	$a\|\|$b or $a or $b	Returns TRUE if either $a or $b are true.
!	NOT	!$a	Returns TRUE if $is not true.

Assignment Operators

Assignment operators are used to assign values to variables. They provide a way to store and update data in variables in PHP. The most commonly used assignment operator is the **basic assignment operator** =, but there are other compound assignment operators that combine assignment with arithmetic operations.

Operator	Name	Example	Operation
=	Assign	$a=$b	The operand on the left gets the value of the operand on the right.
+=	Add then Assign	$a+=$b	Adds the right operand to the left operand and assigns the result to the left operand. Equivalent to $a = $a + $b.
-=	Subtract then Assign	$a-=$b	Subtracts the right operand from the left operand and assigns the result to the left operand. Equivalent to $a = $a - $b.
*=	Multiply then Assign	$a*=$b	Multiplies the left operand by the right operand and assigns the result to the left operand. Equivalent to $a = $a * $b.
/=	Divide then Assign	$a/=$b	Divides the left operand by the right operand and assigns the result to the left operand. Equivalent to $a = $a / $b.

Comparison Operators

Comparison operators (also known as **relational operators**) are used to compare two operands and determine their **relative relationship**. These operators evaluate the relationship between two values, typically returning a Boolean result (true or false) based on whether the comparison is true or false.

Operator	Name	Example	Result
= =	Equal To	$a==$b	Returns True if both operands are equal.
!=	Not Equal To	$a!=$b	Returns True if the operands are not equal.
= = =	Identical	$a= = =$b	Returns true if both operands are equal and of the same type.
!= =	Not Identical	$a!==$b	Returns true if both operands are unequal or of different types.
<	Less than	$a<$b	Returns True if $a is less than $b.
>	Greater Than	$a>$b	Returns True if $a is greater than $b.
<=	Less than or Equal To	$a <= $b	Returns True if $x is less than or equal to $y.
>=	Greater than or Equal To	$a >= $b	Returns True if $x is greater than or equal to $y.

Bitwise Operators

Bitwise operators are used to perform operations on the binary representations of integers. They operate at the bit level, allowing for the manipulation of individual bits within the operands.

Operator	Name	Example	Operation
&	AND	$a&$b	Bits that are set in both $a and $b are set. The result is 1 only if both bits are 1
|	OR	$a\|$b	Bits that are set in either $a or $b are set. The result of OR is 1 if any of the corresponding bits in $a or $b is 1..
^	XOR	$a^$b	Bits that are set in $a or $b, but not both, are set. The result is 1 if exactly one of the bits is 1.
~	NOT	~$a	Bits that are set in $a are cleared, and vice versa. This performs a bitwise complement.
<<	LEFT SHIFT	$a << $b	Shifts the bits of $a left by $b positions. Each shift left multiplies the number by 2.
>>	RIGHT SHIFT	$a>>$b	Shifts the bits of $a right by $b positions. Each shift right divides the number by 2.

Increment/Decrement Operators

Increment operators are used to increase a variable's value by one, while decrement operators are used to decrease a variable's value by one.

Operator	Name	Description
++$a	Pre Increment	Increments $a by one, then returns the new value of $a.
--$a	Pre Decrement	Decrements $a by one, then returns the new value of $a.
$a++	Post Increment	Returns the current value of $a, then increments $a by one
$a--	Post Decrement	Returns the current value of $a, then decrements $a by one.

1.6.2   Expressions

An **expression** in programming is a combination of variables, constants, operators, and function calls that are evaluated to produce a value. In PHP, expressions can be simple, like a mathematical calculation or a string concatenation, or they can be more complex, involving multiple operators and function calls.

Key Characteristics of Expressions:

1. **Evaluates to a Value**: An expression always results in a value, which can be a number, string, boolean, array, or object.

2. **Components**: Expressions can include:

   o **Variables**: Represent data values.

   o **Operators**: Such as arithmetic (+, -), comparison (==, !=), and logical (&&, ||).

   o **Literals**: Fixed values like numbers or strings.

   o **Function Calls**: Invoking functions that return values.

Examples of Expressions:

- **Arithmetic**: 5 + 10 evaluates to 15.
- **String Concatenation**: "Hello" . " World" evaluates to "Hello World".
- **Comparison**: 5 > 3 evaluates to true.

1.7   Constants

A constant is a named data item with a predefined value, that cannot be changed during the execution of the program.

PHP constants can be defined in two ways: using the define( ) function or the const keyword.

1.7.1   Using the define( ) Function:

The define( ) function is used to create a constant at runtime.

Syntax:

define(name, value, case-insensitive) ;

- **name:** specifies the constant name.
- **value:** specifies the constant value.
- **case-insensitive:** Optional parameter; if set to true, the constant name will be case-insensitive. The default is false (case-sensitive).

1.7.2   Program: Creating a Constant in PHP Using define( )

```php
<?php
// Case-sensitive constant name
define('MESSAGE', 'Welcome to PHP');
// Output the value of the constant
echo MESSAGE;
?>
```

1.7.3   Using const keyword

PHP introduced the const keyword to create constants. The const keyword defines constants at compile time. It is a language construct, not a function. Constants defined using the const keyword are case-sensitive by default.

1.7.4   Program: Define a constant using the const keyword

```php
<?php
const PI = 3.14159;
// Output the value of the constant
echo PI; // Outputs: 3.14159
?>
```

1.7.5   Understanding the Differences: Constants and Variables

Aspect	Constants	Variables
Redefinition	Once defined, cannot be redefined or changed.	Can be defined and redefined easily.
Definition	Defined using define() function or const keyword. Cannot be defined by simple assignment.	Defined by simple assignment (=) operator.
Syntax	No dollar ($) sign before the name.	Requires a dollar ($) sign before the name.
Example	define('NAME','value'); const NAME = 'value';	$variableName = 'value';
Scope	Global by default; can be accessed anywhere.	Can be local, global, or static, following scoping rules.
Mutability	Value cannot be changed once set.	Value can be changed throughout the program.
Scoping Rules	No scoping rules; constants are globally accessible.	Must follow variable scoping rules (local, global, static).

1.8 Keywords:

PHP has a set of reserved keywords that cannot be used as function names, variable names, class names, or method names. These keywords are predefined by the PHP language and have special meaning or functions within the language. Examples of PHP keywords include If, do, while, echo, else, case…… etc

These reserved words are crucial for PHP's syntax and functionality. Therefore, they should not be used as names for functions, variables, classes, or methods to avoid conflicts and maintain code clarity.

FLOW CONTROL FUNCTIONS IN PHP

Introduction

Control statements in PHP are essential tools that determine the flow of a program based on specific conditions or logic. They enable decision-making, repetition of tasks, and selective code execution, making your scripts dynamic and responsive.

These statements allow a PHP script to execute certain blocks of code only when specific conditions are met. By using control statements, developers can create programs that adapt to various scenarios, such as user input or data processing.

Control statements are integral to PHP programming as they provide mechanisms to handle different logical paths and repetitions within the code. Without them, a PHP script would execute linearly, lacking the ability to make decisions or repeat actions based on dynamic conditions. Mastering these control structures enables developers to write sophisticated, flexible, and maintainable code, enhancing PHP's power as a tool for web development.

Control statements: Control statements help to determine the order of execution of instructions in a program. They can be categorized into three types:

- Conditional/Selection statements.
- Iteration/Loop statements.
- Jump statements.

2.1   Conditional/Selection statements

Conditional statements are executed based on whether a specific condition or set of conditions is fulfilled.

In PHP, primarily there are four types of conditional control statements used to control the flow of execution based on conditions:

2.1.1   Simple if:

The **if** statement executes a block of code, if the condition is true.

The if statement is a fundamental control structure that allows to execute a block of code only when a specified condition is met. It's the simplest form of conditional statement and is widely used to make decisions in a program based on dynamic data or user input.

Syntax:

```
if (condition)
{
    // Code to be executed if the condition is true
}
```

A condition is an expression that evaluates to either true or false. If the condition is true, the code block inside the if statement is executed. If the condition is false, the code block is skipped.

Program 2.1: Check if the Number is Even

```php
<?php
echo "Enter a number: ";
// Read input from the user
$number = readline();
$number = (int)$number;
if ($number % 2 == 0)
{
   echo $number . " is an even number.";
}
?>
```

The if statement is the cornerstone of conditional logic in PHP, and understanding how to use it effectively is crucial for writing robust and flexible code.

2.1.2   if...else:

The **if...else** statement executes one block of code if a condition is true, and a different block of code if that condition is false.

The **if...else** statement in PHP is an extension of the basic **if** statement. It allows for the execution of one block of code if a condition is true and a different block of code if the condition is false. This structure is useful for handling two possible outcomes based on a condition.

Syntax:

```
if (condition)
{
    // Code to execute if the condition is true
}
else
{
    // Code to execute if the condition is false
}
```

The above syntax consists of a condition, an if block, and an else block.

Components of if...else:

- **condition:** This is an expression that is evaluated to determine if it's true or false.

- **if block:** The code inside this block runs only if the condition evaluates to true.

- **else block:** The code inside this block runs only if the condition evaluates to false.

Program 2.1.2: Check if the Number is Even or Odd

```php
<?php
echo "Enter a number: ";

// Read input from the user
$number = readline();

// Convert the input to an integer
$number = (int)$number;

// Check if the number is even or odd
if ($number % 2 == 0)
{
    echo $number . " is an even number.";
}
else
{
    echo $number . " is an odd number.";
}
?>
```

The if...else statement is a fundamental tool in PHP that allows control over the flow of a program based on conditions, ensuring that the appropriate code is executed depending on the situation.

2.1.3   else if ladder

The else if ladder in PHP allows for multiple conditions to be evaluated in sequence. This construct enables the execution of different actions based on different conditions

The elseif statement in PHP is used to handle multiple conditions within a single control structure. It allows checking a series of conditions one after another, executing the corresponding block of code for the first condition that evaluates to true. This is particularly useful when making decisions based on more than two possible outcomes.

Syntax:

```
if (condition1)
{
    // Code to execute if condition1 is true
}
else if (condition2)
{
    // Code to execute if condition1 is false and condition2 is true
}
 else if (condition3)
{
    // Code to execute if condition1 and condition2 are false and
condition3 is true
}
else
{
    // Code to execute if none of the above conditions are true
}
```

In the above syntax, there are condition1, condition2, condition3, an if block, elseif blocks, and an else block:

- **condition1, condition2, condition3**: These are expressions evaluated in order. The first condition that evaluates to true will trigger its corresponding code block to execute, while the rest will be skipped.

- **if block**: This block is executed if condition1 is true.

- **else if blocks**: These blocks are executed if their respective conditions are true and all preceding conditions have been false.

- **else block**: This block is executed if none of the preceding conditions are true.

Key Points:
- Use the elseif ladder when you need to evaluate multiple conditions and make decisions based on them.
- Each elseif is associated with a preceding if statement, creating a sequence of checks.
- Conditions are evaluated from top to bottom.

- When a condition is true, its corresponding block of code executes, and the remaining conditions are skipped.

- If a condition is false, the next condition is evaluated.

- This process continues until a true condition is found or all conditions are checked.

- If none of the conditions are true, the final else block (if present) executes.

Program 2.1.3: Determine the Grade using an else if ladder

```php
<?php
// Read input from the user
echo "Enter your score: ";
$score = readline();
// Convert the input to an integer
$score = (int)$score;
// Determine the grade using an else if ladder
if ($score >= 90)
{
    echo "Grade: A";
}
else if ($score >= 80)
{
    echo "Grade: B";
}
else if ($score >= 70)
{
    echo "Grade: C";
}
else if ($score >= 60)
{
    echo "Grade: D";
}
else
{
    echo "Grade: F";
}
?>
```

The if...elseif...else statement provides a clear and structured way to handle complex decision-making scenarios in PHP, where multiple conditions need to be evaluated in sequence. This makes the code more readable and easier to maintain when dealing with multiple possible outcomes.

2.1.4 Nested If:

Nested If in PHP Programming is placing if Statement inside another if Statement. A **nested if** statement in PHP is when one if statement is placed inside another if statement. This allows for more complex decision-making processes, where a condition is checked only if a previous condition has already been met. It's particularly useful when the outcome depends on multiple layers of conditions.

Syntax:

The basic syntax of a nested if statement in PHP is as follows:

```php
if (condition1)
{
    // Code to execute if condition1 is true
    if (condition2)
    {
        // Code to execute if condition2 is true
    } else
    {
        // Code to execute if condition2 is false
    }
} else
{
    // Code to execute if condition1 is false
}
```

Key Points:

- **Outer if Statement**: The outer if statement checks the primary condition.

- **Inner if Statement**: The inner if statement is nested inside the block of the outer if and checks a secondary condition if the outer condition is true.

- **else Clauses**: Both the outer and inner if statements can have corresponding else clauses to handle cases where their respective conditions are false.

Program 2.1.4: Find the largest number using nested if statements

```php
<?php
$number1 = 10;
$number2 = 20;
$number3 = 15;
if ($number1 >= $number2)
{
    if ($number1 >= $number3)
    {
        echo "The largest number is $number1.";
    } else
    {
        echo "The largest number is $number3.";
    }
    } else
    {
    if ($number2 >= $number3)
    {
        echo "The largest number is $number2.";
    } else
    {
        echo "The largest number is $number3.";
    }
}
?>
```

Nested if statements in PHP allow for the creation of complex, multi-layered logic, providing precise control over the flow of execution based on multiple conditions. However, it's essential to use them judiciously to maintain code readability and avoid overly complicated logic.

2.1.5   Switch:

In PHP, the switch statement is a control structure that allows to execute one block of code from multiple possible blocks based on the value of an expression

The switch statement in PHP is a control structure that executes one block of code from multiple options based on the value of a variable or expression. It offers an efficient way to manage multiple conditional paths, particularly when several conditions relate to a single variable or expression. The switch statement is often used as an alternative to multiple if...elseif statements.

Syntax:

```
switch (expression)
{
    case value1:
        // Code to execute if expression equals value1
        break;
    case value2:
        // Code to execute if expression equals value2
        break;
    // Add more cases as needed
    default:
        // Code to execute if expression doesn't match any case
        break;
}
```

In the above syntax, there is an 'expression', 'case value', 'break', 'default' parts are there. Functions of these are explained below,

- **expression**: This is the variable or expression that is evaluated once by the switch statement.

- **case value**: Each case checks if the expression matches value. If it does, the corresponding block of code is executed.

- **break**: The break statement ends the execution of the switch block. Without break, the code will continue to execute the subsequent cases even if a match has been found (this is known as "fall-through").

- **default**: The default case is optional and executes if none of the case values match the expression. It's like the else in an if...else statement.

Important Points to be noted about "switch" statement:
- Each case can have a break statement, which is used to terminate the case statement.
- There can be only one default in a switch statement. More than one default may lead to a fatal error.

- The switch statement is a multiway branch statement.
- There can be at least **one or N** number of cases.
- The values in the case must be unique.
- Each statement of the case can have a break statement. It is optional.
- The default statement is also optional

Program 2.1.5: Switch statement to display the day of the week

```php
<?php
$dayNumber = 3;
switch ($dayNumber)
{
    case 1:
        echo "Monday";
        break;
    case 2:
        echo "Tuesday";
        break;
    case 3:
        echo "Wednesday";
        break;
    case 4:
        echo "Thursday";
        break;
    case 5:
        echo "Friday";
        break;
    case 6:
        echo "Saturday";
        break;
    case 7:
        echo "Sunday";
        break;
    default:
        echo "Invalid day number. Please enter a number between 1
and 7.";
        break;
}
?>
```

The switch statement in PHP is a powerful tool that simplifies decision-making when a variable or expression needs to be compared against multiple possible values. It enhances code readability and maintainability, especially when handling a large number of conditions.

2.2 Iteration/Loop statements

Iteration, or looping, is a fundamental concept in PHP that allows for the repeated execution of a block of code based on specific conditions. Loop statements are essential in programming as they enable tasks such as processing data collections, automating repetitive operations, and simplifying complex logic by systematically handling tasks.

Advantages of Loop Statements

1. **Repetition**: The core idea of loops is repetition. With loops, you can repeat the same block of code multiple times without writing it out explicitly for each repetition. This is particularly useful when working with arrays, lists, or any kind of data that requires the same operation to be applied to each element.

2. **Condition-Based Execution**: Loops typically continue running as long as a specified condition remains true. Once the condition is no longer met, the loop stops. This allows you to control the number of iterations dynamically based on the data or user input.

3. **Efficiency**: By using loops, you can perform repetitive tasks more efficiently, both in terms of coding and runtime performance. For instance, instead of writing code to process each item in an array individually, a loop can handle all items in a few lines of code.

Various types of iteration or loop statements are explained below,

2.2.1 while Loop:

The while loop in PHP repeatedly executes a block of code as long as a specified condition evaluates to true. It checks the condition before executing the loop's body. This control structure is particularly useful when the number of iterations is not known in advance and depends on the condition being evaluated during each iteration.

Syntax:

The basic syntax of a while loop can be written as,

```
while(condition)
{
//set of code;
}
```

In the above syntax, there is a 'condition' which can perform as below,

condition: An expression that is evaluated before each iteration. If the condition evaluates to true, the loop executes the code block. If it evaluates to false, the loop terminates, and the program continues with the code following the loop.

Program 2.2.1: PHP Program to Print Fibonacci Sequence Using while Loop

```php
<?php
$terms = 10;

$first = 0;
$second = 1;

$count = 0;

echo "Fibonacci sequence:\n";

while ($count < $terms)
{
    echo $first . " ";

    $next = $first + $second;

    $first = $second;
    $second = $next;

    $count++;
}
?>
```

The while loop in PHP is a versatile and powerful tool for handling scenarios where the number of iterations is not known in advance. By understanding and effectively using the while loop, you can manage repetitive tasks and dynamic conditions in your PHP applications.

2.2.2   Do while loop:

The do...while loop in PHP is a variation of the while loop that guarantees the code block will be executed at least once, regardless of whether the condition evaluates to true initially. This is because the condition is checked after the code block is executed. This makes the do...while loop particularly useful when you need to ensure that a block of code runs at least once before checking a condition.

Syntax:

The syntax of the do...while loop is:

```
do
{
    // Code to be executed at least once and repeatedly while the
condition is true
} while (condition);
```

Code Block: The block of code inside the do section is executed once before the condition is evaluated.

condition: After executing the code block, the condition is checked. If the condition evaluates to true, the loop executes the code block again. If it evaluates to false, the loop terminates, and the program continues with the code following the loop.

Program 2.2.2: PHP Program to Print Natural Numbers Using do...while Loop

```php
<?php
$n = 10;
  $count = 1;
do
{
    echo "$count\n";
    $count++;
} while ($count <= $n);
?>
```

2.2.3   For loop:

A "for loop" is a repetition control structure that allows you to execute a loop a specific number of times efficiently. It is an entry-controlled loop where the initialization, condition, and update statements are included in its syntax.

In PHP, the for loop is used for iterating over a block of code a predetermined number of times. It is ideal for scenarios where the number of iterations is known in advance. The for loop provides a concise way to initialize a counter, set a condition, and update the counter, all in a single line, making it a powerful tool for controlled repetition.

Syntax:

The syntax of the for loop is:

```php
for (initialization; condition; increment)
{
    // Code to be executed in each iteration
}
```

The syntax of the for loop is explained below,

- **initialization**: This expression is executed once at the beginning of the loop. It is typically used to initialize a loop counter or variable.

- **condition**: This expression is evaluated before each iteration. If it evaluates to true, the code block inside the loop is executed. If it evaluates to false, the loop terminates.

- **increment/decrement**: This expression is executed after each iteration. It is used to update the loop counter, typically by incrementing or decrementing it.

Program 2.2.3: PHP script for printing the multiplication table.

```php
<?php
// Get the number from user input
$number = readline("Enter a number: ");
// Check if the input is a valid number
if (!is_numeric($number))
{
    echo "Please enter a valid number.\n";
    exit;
}
// Convert input to integer
$number = (int)$number;

// Loop to print the multiplication table
for ($i = 1; $i <= 10; $i++)
{
    echo $number . " * " . $i . " = " . ($number * $i) . "\n";
}
?>
```

The for loop in PHP is a versatile and powerful tool for scenarios where the number of iterations is known in advance. By using it effectively, you can concise and efficient code for repetitive tasks and data processing can be written.

2.2.4   Nested loops:

Nested loops in PHP refer to the practice of placing one loop inside another. This allows you to perform more complex iterations, such as processing multi-dimensional arrays or creating complex patterns. Nested loops are commonly used in scenarios where you need to iterate over a data structure that contains multiple layers or dimensions.

A nested loop is essentially a loop inside another loop, and the inner loop executes completely for each iteration of the outer loop.

Syntax:

The syntax for nested loops is essentially the same as for single loops. place one loop inside the block of code of another loop.

```
for (initialization; condition; increment)
{
    // Outer loop code

    for (initialization; condition; increment)
{
        // Inner loop code
    }

    // More outer loop code
}
```

Example for nested loop program is given below,

Program 2.2.4: Nested Loops

```php
<?php
// The outer loop runs 3 times, and for each iteration of the outer loop,
// the inner loop runs 2 times.

for ($i = 1; $i <= 3; $i++)
{
    echo "Outer loop iteration: $i\n";

    // Inner loop
    for ($j = 1; $j <= 2; $j++)
{
        echo "  Inner loop iteration: $j\n";
    }
}
?>
```

2.3   Jumping Statements

In PHP, jumping statements are used to control the flow of execution within loops or conditional structures. These statements can alter the sequence of code execution, allowing you to skip over certain parts of a loop, exit loops prematurely, or continue execution from a specific point. The primary jumping statements in PHP are break, continue, and goto. Each serves a different purpose.

2.3.1   break Statement in PHP:

The break statement in PHP is used to exit from a loop or a switch statement prematurely. It terminates the execution of the nearest enclosing loop or switch, and control is transferred to the first statement that follows the loop or switch. This allows you to stop the loop's execution based on a condition, rather than iterating through all the iterations.

Usage of Break statement in a loop is shown in the below Program:

Program 2.3.1: a Usage of "Break" in a Loop

```php
<?php
for ($i = 1; $i <= 5; $i++)
{
    if ($i == 3)
    {
        break; // Exits the loop when $i equals 3
    }
    echo "Iteration: $i\n";
}
?>
```

Program 2.3.1: b Usage of "Break" in a Switch

```php
<?php
$day = 3;

switch ($day)
{
    case 1:
        echo "Monday\n";
        break;
    case 2:
        echo "Tuesday\n";
        break;
    case 3:
        echo "Wednesday\n";
        break;
    default:
        echo "Invalid day\n";
        break;
}
?>
```

2.3.2   continue Statement in PHP:

The continue statement in PHP is used to skip the remaining code in the current iteration of a loop and proceed with the next iteration. It effectively skips over any code that follows it within the loop's block, based on a specific condition. This can be useful when certain iterations or conditions within the loop to bypass.

Program 2.3.2: (a) Usage of "continue" in a for Loop

```php
<?php
for ($i = 1; $i <= 5; $i++)
{
    if ($i == 3)
    {
        continue; // Skip the rest of this iteration when $i equals 3
    }
    echo "Iteration: $i\n";
}
?>
```

Program 2.3.2: (b) Usage of "continue" in a while Loop

```php
<?php
$i = 1;
while ($i <= 5)
{
    if ($i == 3)
    {
        $i++;
        continue; // Skip the rest of this iteration when $i equals 3
    }
    echo "Iteration: $i\n";
    $i++;
}
?>
```

2.3.3   goto Statement:

The "goto" statement transfers control to a different part of the script, marked by a user-defined label. This can be useful in certain scenarios but should be used sparingly to avoid making the code complex and difficult to follow.

Syntax:

```php
goto label;

// Code before the label

label:
    // Code to execute when jumped to
```

Program 2.3.3: goto Usage

```php
<?php
$i = 1;

start:
    if ($i > 5)
    {
        goto end; // Jump to the 'end' label if $i is greater than 5
    }
    echo "Iteration: $i\n";
    $i++;
    goto start; // Jump back to the 'start' label

end:
    echo "end of loop\n";
?>
```

WORKING WITH FUNCTIONS

Introduction

Functions in PHP are essential building blocks of code that help in organizing, reusing, and managing code efficiently. Functions are designed to perform specific tasks. They encapsulate a set of instructions that can be executed whenever needed, making the code more modular, readable, and maintainable. Here's a detailed introduction to functions in PHP, covering their definition, usage, and key features.

Functions help in breaking down complex problems into smaller, manageable tasks. They make code more modular by allow to group related operations together, which simplifies development and debugging. Once a function is defined, it can be called multiple times from different parts of a program and avoid repetition and making code to be effective. Functions can accept input values (parameters) and can return results. This allows functions to be flexible and to process data dynamically.

3.1   Functions

3.1.1   Definition:

A function is a block of code designed to perform a specific task. It can be used repeatedly in a program and helps in organizing code by encapsulating logic that can be reused.

To define a function in PHP, use the keyword **function** followed by the function›s name, parentheses containing the parameters, and curly braces containing the code block. Parameters can be passed into functions by value or by reference. When passing by reference, the parameter is prefixed with an ampersand (&).

Syntax:

Syntax of the function is shown below,

```
function functionName($param1, $param2, ...)
{
    // Code to execute
    return $result; // Optional
}
```

The above syntax is consisting of a keyword 'function', 'function name', parameters and coding block. These are defined as below,

- **function**: Keyword to define a function.

- **functionName**: Name of the function. It should be descriptive and follow naming conventions.

- **$param1, $param2, ...**: Optional parameters that the function can accept. Parameters are used to pass data to the function.

- **return $result;**: Optional statement that specifies the value to be returned from the function.

There are two types of functions in PHP programming:

built-in functions and
user-defined functions.

3.1.2   Built-in Functions:

PHP built-in functions are pre-defined functions that come with PHP and provide a wide range of functionalities for common programming tasks. These functions are part of PHP's core library and cover various aspects of programming, including string manipulation, array handling, file operations, and more. They are optimized for performance and are a key part of the PHP standard library.

PHP has over 1000 built-in functions that can be called directly from within a script to perform specific tasks.

Example: echo( ), print(), foepn( ), abs( ), round( ), etc.

3.1.3 User-Defined Functions:

User-defined functions in PHP are custom functions created by developers to perform specific tasks. These functions allows to encapsulate a set of instructions into a reusable block, making a code more organized, modular, and easier to maintain. A function will not execute automatically when a page loads. A function is executed when it is called explicitly using a function call.

Points to be noted:

- A function name is followed by an open and closed parenthesis.
- A function is declared using the keyword **function**.
- To call a function, write its name followed by parentheses and a semicolon.
- A function name cannot start with a number; it can start with an alphabet or an underscore.
- Function names are case-insensitive.

3.1.4 Calling Functions:

Calling functions in PHP is the process of executing the code that has been defined within a function. When you call a function, PHP executes the block of code inside that function.

Once a function is defined, you can call it by using its name followed by parentheses. If the function has parameters, you pass the arguments inside the parentheses.

Syntax:
The syntax for "calling a function" is,

```
functionName();
```

In the above syntax,

functionName: The name of the function you want to call.

Parentheses (): Used to invoke the function. If the function requires arguments, they are placed inside these parentheses.

To **call a function** in PHP means to execute the function's code by using its name followed by parentheses. When a function is called, any code within the function's block is executed.

Syntax:

```
functionname();
```

Program 3.1.3: Function Example

```php
<?php
function greet()
{
    echo "hello world";
}
greet();
?>
```

In this example:

- The function greet() is defined without parameters.
- The function is called using greet();, which outputs "Hello, World!".

3.2   Returning values from User-Defined Functions

A function can return a value using the return statement along with a value or object. The return statement stops the execution of the function and sends the value back to the calling code.

Returning values from user-defined functions in PHP is essential for allowing functions to provide data back to the part of the program that invoked them. This capability enables further processing or display of the returned information.

The **return** statement is used within a function to send a value back to the calling code. When a return statement is executed, the function stops executing immediately, and the specified value is returned to the point where the function was called. This makes it possible to use the returned value in expressions, assignments, or other operations in the code.

Syntax:

```
function functionName($parameters)
{
    // Code to execute
    return $value;
}
```

$value: The value that you want to return from the function. This can be of any type (e.g., string, integer, array, object, etc.).

Program 3.2.1 (a): Program to add two numbers using a function and display the result

```php
<?php
function addFunction($num1, $num2)
{
    $sum = $num1 + $num2;
    return $sum;
}
$value = addFunction(10, 20);
echo "Returned value from the function: $value";
?>
```

For returning more than one value, function cannot directly return more than one value. However, it can return multiple values by encapsulating them in an array or an object. This approach allows you to package multiple pieces of data and return them as a single entity. Therefore, to return more than one value from a function, use an array.

For example: return array(1, 2, 3, 4);

Program 3.2.1 (b): Program to return multiple values from a function using an array

```php
<?php
// Define the function that returns multiple values
function getDetails()
{
    $name = "John";
    $age = 30;
    $city = "New York";
    // Return multiple values as an array
    return array($name, $age, $city);
}
// Call the function and store the returned values
$details = getDetails();

// Access and display the returned values
echo "Name: " . $details[0] . "<br>";
echo "Age: " . $details[1] . "<br>";
echo "City: " . $details[2] . "<br>";
?>
```

3.3   Arguments in Functions

The information or variables within the function's parentheses are called arguments. These arguments are used to accept inputs during runtime. A user can specify as many arguments as needed, separated by commas. Arguments can be passed to a function when it is called and provide the function with the specific data it needs to perform it's task.

Syntax:

```php
function functionName($param1, $param2, ...)
{
    // Code to execute using $param1, $param2, ...
}
```

In the above syntax, '$param1, $param2, ...: are the parameters that the function expects.

Here's a simple example of a function that takes two arguments:

Program 3.3.1: Add two numbers and display the result

```php
<?php
function addFunction($num1, $num2)
{
    $sum = $num1 + $num2;
    echo "Sum of the two numbers is: " . $sum;
}
addFunction(10, 20);
?>
```

3.4   Parameter Passing in Functions

In PHP, passing parameters to function can be done in two ways, they are,

- Pass (Call) by value
- Pass by reference

3.4.1   Pass (Call) by Value: (Default Behavior)

When you pass a parameter by value in PHP, the function receives a copy of the variable's data. As a result, any modifications made to this parameter within the function do not alter the original variable outside the function.

Points to be noted:
- In call by value, the values of actual parameters are copied to the function's formal parameters.
- There are two copies of parameters stored in different memory locations: one for the actual parameters and one for the formal parameters.
- Changes made to the formal parameters do not affect the actual parameters in the caller.
- PHP supports call by value by default.

Program 3.4.1: Call by value

```php
<?php
function addFunction($num1, $num2)
{
    $sum = $num1 + $num2;
    echo "Sum of the two numbers is: " . $sum;
}
addFunction(10, 20);
?>
```

3.4.2   Call by Reference:

The call by reference method of passing parameters to a function copies the address of an actual parameter into the formal parameter. Inside the function, this address is used to access and modify the actual parameter. As a result, changes made to the formal parameter will affect the actual parameter.

Note: In the below code, the '&' symbol before the parameter in the function definition indicates that the parameter is passed by reference.

Program 3.4.2: Call by Reference Example

```php
<?php
// Function to increment a variable by reference
function increment(&$i)
{
    $i++;
}
// Initialize the variable
$i = 10;
// Call the function with the variable passed by reference
increment($i);
// Output the incremented value
echo $i;
?>
```

3.5 Saving State Between Function Calls with the Static Statement

working with functions in PHP, you might need to preserve the value of a variable between multiple function calls. This can be achieved using the **static** keyword.

The static keyword in PHP is used within a function to declare a variable that retains its value between function calls. Unlike regular local variables, which are reinitialized every time the function is called, a static variable maintains its state across calls. This is useful when you want a variable to persist across multiple executions of the function without being reset.

Syntax for saving the state of the variable with static keyword is,

Syntax:

```
function function_name()
{
    static $variable = initial_value;
    // Function code that modifies $variable
}
```

Program 3.5: Saving state between Function calls

```
<?php
function counter()
{
    static $count = 0; // Initialize a static variable
    $count++;
    echo "Counter: $count\n";
}
counter(); // Outputs: Counter: 1
counter(); // Outputs: Counter: 2
counter(); // Outputs: Counter: 3
?>
```

In the above example,

- **static $count = 0;:** The static keyword is used to declare the $count variable. Unlike a regular variable, which is reinitialized each time the function is called, a static variable retains its value across multiple calls to the function.

- **First Call**: When counter() is called for the first time, $count is initialized to 0 and then incremented to 1.
- **Subsequent Calls**: On the second and third calls, the value of $count continues from where it left off, incrementing by 1 each time.

3.6   Variable Scope

In PHP, the scope of a variable determines where the variable can be accessed and modified within the code. the scope of a variable refers to the context within which a variable is accessible and can be used. The scope determines where a variable is visible and how long it exists during the execution of a script.

3.6.1   Global Scope

Variables declared outside of functions are in the global scope. They can be accessed from anywhere in the script except inside functions, unless explicitly imported.

If global variables are declared outside of any function or method, they can be accessed inside a function using the keyword global.

The global keyword allows functions to access variables declared outside their scope, but it must be used correctly within the function.

global scope nature can be understood by the following code,

```php
$globalVar = "I'm global!";
function myFunction()
{
    echo $globalVar; // Error: Undefined variable
}
myFunction();
echo $globalVar; // Outputs: I'm global!
```

In the above code, the variable $globalVar is globally accessible outside any function. However, it is not directly accessible inside myFunction() unless you use the global keyword. That is why it shown error when it tries to access inside the function.

It can be accessed within the function successfully by using the keyword 'global'. This code is shown below,

```php
$globalVar = "I'm global!";
function myFunction()
{
    global $globalVar;
    echo $globalVar; // Outputs: I'm global!
}
myFunction();
```

Program 3.6.1: Global Scope

```php
<?php
$g = "I am a global variable"; // Global variable
function display()
{
    global $g; // Access the global variable
    echo $g; // Output the value of the global variable
}
display(); // Output: I am a global variable
?>
```

3.6.2   Local Scope:

Variables declared within a function are considered to have local scope. These variables can only be accessed within the function where they are defined.

Local scope of the variable can be understood by the following code,

```php
function myFunction()
{
    $localVar = "I'm local!";
    echo $localVar;
}
myFunction(); // Outputs: I'm local!
echo $localVar; // Error: Undefined variable
```

$localVar is only available inside myFunction(). Attempting to access it outside the function will result in an error.

Program 3.6.2: Local scope

```php
<?php
function display()
{
    $l = "I am a local variable";
    echo $l;
}
display(); // Output: I am a local variable
?>
```

3.6.3   Static Scope

Variables declared with the static keyword inside a function retain their value between function calls. This is useful for preserving state across multiple calls to the same function.

Example code for static scope is given below,

```php
function myCounter()
{
    static $count = 0;
    $count++;
    echo $count;
}
myCounter(); // Outputs: 1
myCounter(); // Outputs: 2
myCounter(); // Outputs: 3
```

The '$count' variable is initialized only once, and its value is preserved across subsequent calls to 'myCounter()'.

Program 3.6.3: Static Scope

```php
<?php
function visitCounter()
{
    // Declare a static variable
    static $count = 0;

    // Increment the counter
    $count++;

    // Output the current value of the counter
    echo "This function has been called $count times.<br>";
}

// Call the function multiple times
visitCounter(); // Outputs: This function has been called 1 times.
visitCounter(); // Outputs: This function has been called 2 times.
visitCounter(); // Outputs: This function has been called 3 times.
visitCounter(); // Outputs: This function has been called 4 times.
?>
```

WORKING WITH ARRAYS AND STRINGS

Introduction:

In the world of programming, managing data efficiently is key to building robust and scalable applications. As a developer, you often need to work with groups of related data, like lists of products, names, or even more complex data structures. Instead of handling each piece of data as a separate variable, PHP provides a powerful and flexible tool to group and organize data with the help of **arrays**.

4.1   Arrays:

An **array** in PHP is a special variable that allows you to store multiple values in a single container. Instead of creating multiple variables for each item, you can use an array to store all the related data together. This not only makes your code cleaner but also easier to maintain and manipulate.

PHP arrays are highly versatile and can hold a variety of data types, including integers, strings, and even other arrays. In fact, arrays are one of the most commonly used data structures in PHP because of their flexibility and ease of use.

Why Learn Arrays?

Understanding arrays is crucial because they:

- **Simplify Data Handling**: You can store, sort, and manipulate large sets of data with ease.

- **Enhance Code Efficiency**: Instead of writing repetitive code, arrays let you use loops and array functions to perform operations on data sets.

- **Allow Dynamic Data Storage**: PHP arrays are dynamic, meaning you don't need to declare the size or type of the array beforehand. You can add or remove elements at any time.

Real-world Examples of Arrays

Arrays are used in a wide range of real-world applications, such as:

- **E-commerce**: Managing a list of products or a shopping cart.
- **Web Forms**: Handling multiple inputs from users.
- **Database Results**: Storing and processing rows of data retrieved from a database query.

In this chapter, we will explore the different types of arrays in PHP, how to create and manipulate them, and how to use array-related functions to perform common tasks. By the end of this chapter, you will have a solid understanding of arrays and be ready to apply them in your PHP projects.

Syntax for Arrays:

In PHP, arrays are defined using the array() function or using short array syntax []. Both methods work the same way, and PHP allows you to store multiple values in a single variable. Arrays can store values of any type, such as integers, strings, or even other arrays.

Example for creating an array in two ways as,

```php
// Using the array() function
$fruits = array("Apple", "Banana", "Orange");
// Using the short array syntax
$fruits = ["Apple", "Banana", "Orange"];
```

Program 4.1: An Array Holding Different Data Types

```php
<?php
// An array holding different data types
$myArray = array(1, "Hello", 3.14, true);
// Accessing array elements
echo $myArray[0]; // Outputs: 1
echo $myArray[1]; // Outputs: Hello
?>
```

4.2   Types of Arrays:
PHP supports three types of arrays as mentioned below,

1.   Indexed Arrays

2.   Associative Arrays

3.   Multidimensional Arrays

4.2.1   Indexed Arrays
Indexed arrays are arrays in which each element is assigned an automatically incremented numeric index, starting from 0. They are ideal for storing lists of data where the order of elements is significant

Syntax:
Using the array() Function,: An older method for creating arrays, compatible with all PHP versions.

```php
// Using the array() function
$indexedArray = array(value1, value2, value3);


// Using shorthand syntax (PHP 5.4 and later)
$indexedArray = [value1, value2, value3];
```

Example:

```php
$colors = array("red", "green", "blue");
```

Here, the array $colors has three elements:

```php
$colors[0] = "Red"
$colors[1] = "Green"
$colors[2] = "Blue"
```

Accessing Elements: Elements in the indexed array can accessed using the index number

```php
echo $colors[0]; // Outputs: red
echo $colors[1]; // Outputs: green
echo $colors[2]; // Outputs: blue
```

Adding Elements: Elements can be added to an indexed array without specifying an index.

```php
$colors[] = "Yellow";
Now,
$colors[3] = "Yellow".
```

Program 4.2.1: program for Indexed Arrays

```php
<?php
// Program 4.1.1: Example of Indexed Arrays Access
$c = array(10, 20, 30);   // Create an indexed array with three
elements
echo "$c[0]\n";  // Output the first element of the array with a
newline
echo "$c[1]\n";  // Output the second element of the array with a
newline
echo $c[2];     // Output the third element of the array
?>
```

4.2.2   Associative Arrays:

Associative arrays use named keys to store data instead of numeric indexes. This makes them perfect for storing data in key-value pairs where the key is a string. or

Arrays with Named Keys. Arrays where each key is associated with a specific value. Keys are named explicitly and can be strings or numbers.

Syntax for creating an Associative Arrays

Using array() function to define an associative array with named keys.

```
$array_name = array( key1 => value1,key2 => value2, key3 => value3,..);
```

Parameter values:

Parameter	Description
Key	The name used to identify the array element.
Value	The data associated with the key.

Here ,an example is given,

```
$person = array("name" => "John", "age" => 30, "city" => "New York");
```

Here, the array $person has three key-value pairs:

- "name" => "John"
- "age" => 30
- "city" => "New York"

You can access elements of an associative array using the key.

```
echo $person["name"]; // Outputs: John
echo $person["age"];  // Outputs: 30
```

You can add elements to an associative array by specifying a new key-value pair.

```
$person["country"] = "USA";
Now, $person["country"] = "USA".
```

Program 4.2.2: Program for an Associative Arrays

```php
<?php
$person = array(
    "first_name" => "John",
    "last_name" => "Doe",
    "age" => 30
);
echo "First Name: " . $person["first_name"] . "\n";
echo "Last Name: " . $person["last_name"] . "\n";
echo "Age: " . $person["age"];
?>
```

4.2.3   Multidimensional Arrays

A multidimensional array is an array that contains one or more arrays as its elements. It is also known as an "array of arrays". They are useful for storing complex data structures, such as matrices or tabular data.

PHP supports multidimensional arrays that can be two, three, four, five, or more levels deep.

Creating a Multidimensional Array:

```php
$people = array(
    "John" => array("age" => 30, "city" => "New York"),
    "Jane" => array("age" => 25, "city" => "Chicago"),
    "Dave" => array("age" => 35, "city" => "Los Angeles")
);
```

Here, the array '$people' contains three associative arrays, each representing a person with their corresponding age and city.

You can access elements in a multidimensional array by chaining the indexes/keys.

```php
echo $people["John"]["city"]; // Outputs: New York
echo $people["Jane"]["age"];  // Outputs: 25
```

You can add elements to a multidimensional array by specifying the keys and values.

```
$people["Mike"] = array("age" => 28, "city" => "Boston");
Now, $people["Mike"] contains the array, array("age" => 28, "city"
=> "Boston").
```

Two-Dimensional Arrays

A two-dimensional array is an array of arrays. It's used to store data in a matrix format, where each element in the array is itself an array. This is particularly useful for representing data in rows and columns, such as a table or a grid.

In other words, it is a matrix or table where each element is itself an array. A three-dimensional array is an array of two-dimensional arrays, and so on.

Program 4.2.3: program for an accessing Elements in a Two-Dimensional Array

```php
<?php
$cars = array( array(12, 22, 18),  array(29, 17, 15));
// Output each element with a newline
echo $cars[0][0], "\n";
echo $cars[0][1], "\n";
echo $cars[0][2], "\n";
echo $cars[1][0], "\n";
echo $cars[1][1], "\n";
echo $cars[1][2];
?>
```

4.2.4   PHP foreach Loop

An alternative to the for loop, the foreach loop is used to traverse the elements of an array or object. It will issue an error if used with variables of other data types.

The 'foreach' loop provides an easy way to iterate over array elements. It operates on the elements themselves rather than their indices, and there is no need to manually increment any values.

The foreach loop in PHP is specifically designed for iterating over arrays. It simplifies the process of looping through each element of an array, without the need to manage counters or worry about array bounds. The 'foreach' statement iterates over all elements in the array, one at a time, starting with the first element and ending with the last one.

i. PHP 'foreach' with Indexed Arrays

To iterate over all elements of an indexed array, you use the following syntax:

The basic syntax of a foreach loop is as follows,

```
foreach ($array as $value)
{
    // Code to execute with $value
}
```

When PHP encounters a foreach statement, it assigns the first element of the array to the variable following the as keyword ($variable).

In each iteration, PHP assigns the next array element to this $variable. The loop continues until PHP has processed all elements in the array, then the loop ends.

Program i: 'foreach' with Indexed Arrays

```
<?php
$color = array("red", "green", "yellow");
foreach ($color as $c)
{
    echo $c . "\n";   // Output each color with a newline
}
?>
```

ii. PHP foreach with an Associative Array

To iterate over elements of an associative array, you use the following syntax:

Syntax:

```php
foreach ($array as $key => $value)
{
    // Code to execute with $key and $value
}
```

When PHP encounters the foreach statement, it accesses the first element and assigns:

- The key of the element to the $key variable.

- The value of the element to the $value variable.

Program ii: 'foreach' with an Associative Array

```php
<?php
$person = array("first_name" => "John","last_name" => "Doe","age" => 30);
foreach ($person as $key => $value)
{
    echo "$key: $value\n";   // Output key and value with a newline
}
?>
```

4.3   Strings

Strings in PHP are sequences of characters, used to store and manipulate text. PHP provides a wide range of functions to work with strings, making it a versatile language for handling text. Strings can be created using single quotes (' ') or double quotes (" ").

Single quoted string:

Single-quoted strings are the simplest form. Everything inside the quotes is treated literally, except for the escape sequences '\'' and '\\'.

```php
$greeting = 'Hello, world!';
```

If you need to include a single quote within a single-quoted string, you should escape it with a backslash '\'.

```php
$quote = 'It\'s a beautiful day!';
```

Double-Quoted Strings

Double-quoted strings allow for variable interpolation and interpretation of special escape sequences like '\n' (newline), '\t' (tab), etc.

```php
$name = "John";
$greeting = "Hello, $name!";
echo $greeting; // Outputs: Hello, John!
```

In this example, the variable '$name' is interpolated within the string.

Program 4.3: Usage of Strings in PHP:

```php
<?php
$s = 'hello world';
// Define a string using double quotes
$d = "hello world";
// Output the strings
echo $s;
echo "\n";  // Newline for separation
echo $d;
?>
```

4.4   Formatting Strings with PHP

In PHP, formatting strings involves manipulating and arranging text to achieve a desired output. PHP provides several ways to format strings, ranging from basic concatenation to more advanced techniques like using the printf() and sprintf() functions, as well as string interpolation.

In PHP, string formatting can be accomplished using various methods. Here are some common methods for formatting strings.

4.4.1   Concatenation:

Concatenation is the process of joining two or more strings together to form a single string. In PHP, concatenation is performed using the dot operator (.).

Syntax:

```php
$formattedstring = $string1 . $string2;
```

Here is an example for concatenation,

```php
$firstName = "John";
$lastName = "Doe";
$age = 30;
$formattedString = "My name is " . $firstName . " " . $lastName . "
and I am " . $age . " years old.";
echo $formattedString; // Outputs: My name is John Doe and I am 30
years old.
```

String Interpolation with Double-Quoted Strings

Double-quoted strings in PHP allow you to directly embed variables, making it easy to format strings.

Here is an example for double-Quoted string,

```php
$firstName = "John";
$lastName = "Doe";
$age = 30;
$formattedString = "My name is $firstName $lastName and I am $age
years old.";
echo $formattedString; // Outputs: My name is John Doe and I am 30
years old.
```

Program 4.4.1: Program for String Concatenation

```php
<?php
$first_name = "John";
$last_name = "Doe";
$full_name = $first_name . " " . $last_name;
echo $full_name;   // Output: John Doe
?>
```

sprintf() function:

The sprintf() function in PHP is used to format strings by inserting variables into placeholders within a string. It returns the formatted string without outputting it directly. It is particularly useful when you need to create a string that includes various types of data (such as integers, floating-point numbers, or strings) and you want to control how that data is presented.

Syntax:

The syntax of sprintf() is as follows,

```
sprintf(format, arg1, arg2, ...)
```

- **format**: A string that contains text and format specifiers, which define how each subsequent argument should be formatted.

- **arg1, arg2, ...:** The variables that you want to format according to the format specifiers.

Format Specifiers

Format specifiers start with a percent sign % and are followed by one or more characters that define how the value should be formatted.

Common Format Specifiers

- **%s**: String
- **%d**: Decimal (integer)
- **%f**: Floating-point number
- **%x**: Hexadecimal number (lowercase)

- **%X**: Hexadecimal number (uppercase)
- **%b**: Binary number
- **%%**: A literal percent sign

Program 4.4.2: sprintf() function

```php
<?php
$price = 19.99;
$fprice = sprintf("The price is $%.2f", $price);
echo $fprice;   // Output: The price is $19.99
?>
```

sprintf() in PHP is a powerful function for creating well-formatted strings. It allows you to control the presentation of various data types within a string, making it useful for generating reports, creating user-friendly output, or preparing strings for further processing.

4.4.2   printf():

The printf() function in PHP is used to output a formatted string. It's similar to sprintf(), but instead of returning the formatted string, printf() directly prints it to the output. This function is useful when you need to generate and display a formatted string with variables of different data types.

Syntax:

The syntax of printf() is

```
printf(format, arg1, arg2, ...)
```

- format: A string containing text and format specifiers that determine how the arguments should be formatted.
- arg1, arg2, ...: The variables or values you want to format according to the specified format.

Format Specifiers

Format specifiers are placeholders within the format string that are replaced by the values of the arguments. They start with a percent sign % and are followed by characters that specify the type of data and how it should be formatted.

Common Format Specifiers

- **%s**: String
- **%d**: Decimal (integer)
- **%f**: Floating-point number
- **%x**: Hexadecimal number (lowercase)
- **%X**: Hexadecimal number (uppercase)
- **%b**: Binary number
- **%%**: A literal percent sign

Basic String Formatting example is shown in below,

```php
$name = "Alice";
printf("Hello, %s!", $name); // Outputs: Hello, Alice!
```

In this example, %s is a placeholder for a string, and $name is inserted into the string.

The printf() function in PHP is a powerful tool for creating formatted output. It allows you to control how data is presented, making it useful for generating reports, displaying results in a specific format, or preparing data for output in a user-friendly manner.

Program 4.4.2 printf() Function

```php
<?php
$number = 1234.567;
printf("Number with two decimal places: %.2f", $number);
?>
```

4.4.3 Multiple Variables in printf()

You can include multiple format specifiers in the format string and pass corresponding arguments.

```
$name = "Bob";
$age = 25;
$height = 6.1;


printf("Name: %s, Age: %d, Height: %.1f feet", $name, $age, $height);
// Outputs: Name: Bob, Age: 25, Height: 6.1 feet
```

4.5 Manipulating Strings with PHP

Manipulating strings in PHP is a common task, and PHP provides a rich set of functions to help with this. You can perform a variety of operations on strings, including concatenation, replacing, splitting, joining, trimming, padding, reversing and more.

4.5.1 Concatenation:

Concatenation is the process of joining two or more strings together. In PHP, use the . operator to concatenate strings.

Example:

```
$firstName = "John";
$lastName = "Doe";
$fullName = $firstName . " " . $lastName;
echo $fullName; // Outputs: John Doe
```

4.5.2 Replacing Substrings:

In PHP, the str_replace() function is used to substitute parts of a string with other content. This function can replace all occurrences of a specified substring with a new substring.

Syntax:

```
str_replace(search, replace, subject)
```

Example:

```
$new_text = str_replace("old", "new", $text);
```

- **old**: The substring you want to search for within $text.
- **new**: The substring you want to replace "old" with.
- **$text**: The original string where the replacement will occur.
- **$new_text**: This variable will store the result of the str_replace() operation, which is the modified version of $text with all occurrences of "old" replaced by "new".

4.5.3 Splitting a String into an Array: The explode() function splits a string into an array based on a delimiter.

Syntax : explode(delimiter, string)

Example

```
$text = "apple,banana,orange";
$fruits = explode(",", $text);
print_r($fruits);
// Outputs: Array ( [0] => apple [1] => banana [2] => orange )
```

4.5.4 Joining Array Elements into a String:

The implode() function joins array elements into a single string with a specified delimiter.

```
Syntax: implode(glue, array)
```

Example:

```
$fruits = array("apple", "banana", "orange");
$text = implode(", ", $fruits);
echo $text; // Outputs: apple, banana, orange
```

4.5.5 Trimming Whitespace:
Removing Whitespace from the Start and/or End of a String Using the trim() Function

- **trim()** removes whitespace (or other characters) from the beginning and end of a string.

- **ltrim()** removes whitespace (or other characters) from the beginning of a string.

- **rtrim()** removes whitespace (or other characters) from the end of a string.

Example:

```php
<?php
$text = "Hello, world!    ";
echo trim($text);   // Outputs: Hello, world!
echo ltrim($text);  // Outputs: Hello, world!
echo rtrim($text);  // Outputs: Hello, world!
?>
```

4.5.6 Padding:
The str_pad() function is the primary function for padding strings in PHP. It pads a string to a specified length with another string.

- **Syntax:** str_pad(string, length, pad_string, pad_type)
- **string:** The original string you want to pad.
- **length:** The desired length of the padded string.
- **pad_string:** The string to pad with. This is optional, and if omitted, spaces will be used by default.
- **pad_type:** Specifies where to pad the string. It can be STR_PAD_RIGHT, STR_PAD_LEFT, or STR_PAD_BOTH.

Examples:

Padding to the Right (Default): This will pad the string on the right (end) to reach the specified length.

```php
<?php
$text = "Hello";
$padded = str_pad($text, 10); // Pads with spaces by default
echo $padded; // Outputs: "Hello     " (5 spaces added)
?>
```

Padding to the Left: You can pad the string on the left (beginning) by specifying STR_PAD_LEFT.

```php
<?php
$text = "Hello";
$padded = str_pad($text, 10, "*", STR_PAD_LEFT);
echo $padded; // Outputs: "*****Hello"
?>
```

Padding on Both Sides: If you want to pad the string on both sides (equally if possible), you can use STR_PAD_BOTH.

```php
<?php
$text = "Hello";
$padded = str_pad($text, 10, "-", STR_PAD_BOTH);
echo $padded; // Outputs: "-Hello----" (2 on the left, 3 on the right)
?>
```

4.5.7   Reversing Strings:

The strrev() function is used to reverse the order of characters in a string. This function is straightforward and provides a quick way to reverse a string.

```php
Syntax: $reversed = strrev($text);
```

Example:

```php
<?php
$text = "Hello, world!"; // Define the original string
$reversed = strrev($text); // Reverse the string
echo $reversed; // Outputs: "!dlrow ,olleH"
?>
```

4.6 Investigating Strings with PHP

Investigating strings in PHP involves examining their content, structure, and properties. It focuses on analyzing and understanding the characteristics of strings. This includes measuring length, finding substrings, extracting parts, comparing strings, and checking for the presence of specific substrings.

PHP provides a wide range of functions to analyze and manipulate strings. These functions enable users to determine the length of a string, search for specific characters or substrings, compare strings, and perform various other operations.

4.6.1 Checking String Length:

The strlen() function is used to determine the number of characters in a string. This function returns the length of the string in terms of the number of characters it contains.

Use strlen() to find out the length of a string.

```php
$length = strlen($text);
```

Example:

```php
$str = "Hello, World!";
echo strlen($str); // Outputs: 13
```

4.6.2   Finding a Substring:

strpos() to find the position of the first occurrence of a substring in a string. It returns the index (0-based) of the first match or false if not found.

Example:

```
$str = "Hello, World!";
$pos = strpos($str, "World"); // Outputs: 7
```

4.6.3   Extracting a Substring:

Extracting a substring in PHP is done using the substr() function. This function allows you to retrieve a portion of a string based on a specified starting position and length.

```
Syntax: substr(string $string, int $start, int $length);
```

- **$string**: The input string from which a portion will be extracted.
- **$start**: The starting position of the substring.
- **$length** (optional): The number of characters to extract. If omitted, substr() will return the remainder of the string starting from $start.

Examples:

1.   **Extracting a Substring from a Specified Position**

```
$str = "Hello, World!";
$substring = substr($str, 7, 5); // Extracts "World"
echo $substring;
```

2.   **Extracting from the Beginning**

```
$str = "Hello, World!";
$substring = substr($str, 0, 5); // Extracts "Hello"
echo $substring
```

3. **Extracting to the End of the String:** If you omit the length, substr() will extract from the start position to the end of the string.

```php
$str = "Hello, World!";
$substring = substr($str, 7); // Extracts "World!"
echo $substring;
```

4.6.4 Comparing Strings:

The strcmp() function is used to compare two strings. It returns 0 if the strings are equal, a negative number if the first string is less than the second, and a positive number if the first string is greater. This function performs a case-sensitive comparison of the strings.

Examples:

Program: Comparing Equal Strings

```php
<?php
$str1 = "apple";
$str2 = "apple";

$result = strcmp($str1, $str2);

if ($result == 0)
{
    echo "The strings are equal."; // Outputs: The strings are equal.
} elseif ($result < 0)
{
    echo "$str1 is less than $str2.";
} else
{
    echo "$str1 is greater than $str2.";
}
?>
```

Program: First String is Less Than the Second

```php
<?php
$str1 = "apple";
$str2 = "banana";

$result = strcmp($str1, $str2);

if ($result == 0)
{
    echo "The strings are equal.";
} elseif ($result < 0)
{
    echo "$str1 is less than $str2."; // Outputs: apple is less
than banana.
} else
{
    echo "$str1 is greater than $str2.";
}
?>
```

Program: First String is Greater Than the Second

```php
<?php
$str1 = "banana";
$str2 = "apple";

$result = strcmp($str1, $str2);

if ($result == 0)
{
    echo "The strings are equal.";
} elseif ($result < 0)
{
    echo "$str1 is less than $str2.";
} else
{
    echo "$str1 is greater than $str2."; // Outputs: banana is
greater than apple.
}
?>
```

Program: Case-Sensitive Comparison

```php
<?php
$str1 = "Apple";
$str2 = "apple";

$result = strcasecmp($str1, $str2);

if ($result == 0)
{
    echo "The strings are equal.";
}
 elseif ($result < 0)
{
    echo "$str1 is less than $str2.";
} else
{
    echo "$str1 is greater than $str2.";
}
?>
```

CLASSES AND OBJECTS IN PHP

Introduction

A **class** in PHP serves as a blueprint for creating objects. It encapsulates data for the object and methods to manipulate that data, allowing developers to define the structure and behavior of complex entities. By organizing code into classes, developers can create modular applications that are easier to maintain and extend.

Classes promote the principles of Object-Oriented Programming (OOP) by allowing for encapsulation, where the internal state of an object is protected from outside interference. They can contain properties (variables) that hold data and methods (functions) that define the behavior of the object. This organization helps in modeling real-world concepts in a structured manner, making code more intuitive and reducing redundancy.

An **object** is an instance of a class. When a class is defined, it does not consume memory until an object is created from that class. Objects represent real-world entities and hold data in their properties, while utilizing the methods defined in their class to perform actions.

Creating objects allows developers to use the same structure and behavior defined in a class multiple times, each with its own unique data. This reusability is a cornerstone of OOP, enabling efficient code management and reducing the likelihood of errors. Objects can interact with one another, facilitating complex relationships and behaviors that mirror real-life interactions.

classes and objects are fundamental components of OOP in PHP, enabling the creation of organized, reusable, and maintainable code. By leveraging these concepts, developers can build sophisticated applications that are easier to understand and modify.

Real-Time Applications of Classes and Objects in PHP

1. **Web Development Frameworks:**

   o Frameworks like Laravel and Symfony use classes and objects extensively to organize code, handle routing, and manage database interactions. They promote reusable components and a clear structure, making it easier to develop complex applications.

2. **Content Management Systems (CMS):**

   o Platforms like WordPress and Joomla utilize classes and objects to manage content, user roles, and plugins. Each component, such as posts, pages, and users, can be represented as objects, allowing for efficient content management.

3. **E-commerce Applications:**

   o In e-commerce systems, classes can represent products, customers, orders, and shopping carts. This object-oriented structure enables features like inventory management, user authentication, and payment processing to be developed in a modular way.

4. **Game Development:**

   o In PHP-based games, classes can represent different game entities such as players, enemies, and items. Objects instantiated from these classes can encapsulate behaviors and properties, allowing for dynamic gameplay.

5. **Data Processing Applications:**

   o Applications that process data (like analytics tools) can utilize classes to manage different data types and operations. For instance, classes can represent datasets, analysis methods, and visualization components.

6. **User Authentication Systems:**

   o Classes can be used to handle user accounts, sessions, and permissions. This encapsulation helps in managing user data securely and effectively, making it easier to implement authentication and authorization features.

5.1 Defining a Class

A class in PHP is defined using the 'class' keyword followed by the class name and a pair of curly braces. Inside these braces, you can define properties (variables) and methods (functions) that belong to the class.

A class is a template for objects, and an object is an instance of a class. Multiple instances of the same class can be created.

The class name can be any valid label, provided it is not a PHP reserved word. A valid class name starts with a letter or underscore, followed by any number of letters, numbers, or underscores.

For example, there is a single 'Person' class, but many Person objects can be instances of this class—such as Sony, Tony, Dan etc.

Syntax: We define our own class by starting with the keyword **'class'** followed by the name you want to give your new class.

```php
<?php
    class person
{
    }
?>
```

Here is an example of simple class definition

```php
<?php
class SimpleClass
{
// property declaration
public $var = 'a default value';

// method declaration
public function displayVar()
{
echo $this->var;
}
}
?>
```

In the above example,

- **Properties** are variables defined within a class. They represent the data or state of an object.
- Properties can have different visibility levels (public, protected, private), which control their accessibility.
- **Methods** are functions defined within a class that can operate on the properties and perform actions.
- Like properties, methods can also have visibility levels (public, protected, private).

Note: If you do not specify any access modifier, PHP defaults to public, means that the property or method is accessible from anywhere outside the class.

5.2   Creating Objects

An **object** is an instance of a class. You can create an object using the 'new' keyword.

```
Syntax:   $object_name = new Class_name;
```

Here is an example,

```
$myCar = new Car('Toyota', 'Corolla', 2022);
```

Points to be noted:

- $object_name is the variable that will hold the reference to the newly created object.
- new is the keyword used to create a new instance of the class.
- Class_name is the name of the class from which the object is being created.

5.3   Method Calling

In PHP, **method calling** refers to the process of invoking a method (function) that belongs to a class. This allows an object to perform actions or return information based on its current state or data.

To call a method on an object, use the -> operator to append the method name to the object name. If the method requires arguments, provide them within parentheses. If the method does not require any arguments, use empty parentheses.

Key Ponits:
- Use the -> operator to access a method of the object.
- Provide arguments inside parentheses if the method requires them.
- Use empty parentheses if the method does not require any arguments.

Syntax:

```
$class_name>method_name(); // No arguments    or
$class_name>method_name(value); // Passing an argument
```

Example: For example, if you have an object $myCar and a method startEngine, you would call it like this:

```
$class_name>method_name();
$myCar->startEngine();
```

Program 5.3: Classes and objects example

```php
<?php
class Person
{
    // Define a method within the class
    public function display()
    {
        echo "Hello, world!";
    }
}
// Create a new instance of the Person class
$sony = new Person;
// Call the display method on the $sony object
$sony->display();
?>
```

Keynote:

- The **Person** class is defined with a single method **display()** , which prints "Hello, world!" to the screen. The **public** keyword specifies that the method is accessible from outside the class.

- An object named **Ssony** is created from the Person class using the **new** keyword. This instantiation initializes the object and makes it ready for use.

- The **display()** method of the **$sony** object is called. This executes the code within the **display** method, which outputs "Hello, world!" to the browser.

5.4   Object Instance Working with Strings:

When working with strings in object-oriented PHP, you typically encapsulate string operations within a class, which allows you to manage and manipulate strings in a more organized and reusable manner.

When working with strings using object instances in object-oriented programming (OOP), you handle the strings as follows,

- **Create a Class**: First, you define a class that includes properties and methods to handle strings.

- **Instantiate the Class**: You create an object (an instance of the class).

- **Set String Value**: You assign a string to the object, either when creating it or by using a method.

- **Use Methods to Manipulate the String**: You use the object's methods to perform operations on the string.

5.4.1   Creating a Class to Handle Strings:

To work with strings using an object instance, you first create a class that defines the properties and methods for string manipulation sample code as shown in below example,

Program 5.4.1 creating a class to handle strings

```php
class StringManipulator
{
    private $string; // Property to hold the string
    // Constructor to initialize the string
    public function __construct($string)
    {
        $this->string = $string;
    }
    // Method to convert the string to uppercase
    public function toUpperCase()
    {
        return strtoupper($this->string);
    }
    // Method to convert the string to lowercase
    public function toLowerCase()
    {
        return strtolower($this->string);
    }
    // Method to reverse the string
    public function reverse()
    {
        return strrev($this->string);
    }
    // Method to get the length of the string
    public function length()
    {
        return strlen($this->string);
    }
    // Method to replace a substring with another
    public function replace($search, $replace)
    {
        return str_replace($search, $replace, $this->string);
    }
    // Method to return the current string
    public function getString()
    {
        return $this->string;
    }
    // Method to set a new string
    public function setString($string)
    {
        $this->string = $string;
    }
}
```

5.4.2 Instantiating the Class:

Once the class is defined, you can create an instance of it and manipulate strings through that instance.

```php
// Create an instance of StringManipulator
$stringManipulator = new StringManipulator("Hello World!");
```

5.4.3 Using Methods to Manipulate the String:

Methods can be used which are defined in the class to perform various string operations.

```php
// Convert the string to uppercase
echo $stringManipulator->toUpperCase(); // Outputs: HELLO WORLD!
// Convert the string to lowercase
echo $stringManipulator->toLowerCase(); // Outputs: hello world!
// Reverse the string
echo $stringManipulator->reverse(); // Outputs: !dlroW olleH
// Get the length of the string
echo $stringManipulator->length(); // Outputs: 12
// Replace a substring within the string
echo $stringManipulator->replace("World", "PHP"); // Outputs: Hello PHP!
```

Program 5.4: PHP program for Object Instance Working with Strings

```php
<?php
class StringManipulator
{
    private $string; // Property to hold the string

    // Constructor to initialize the string
    public function __construct($string)
    {
        $this->string = $string;
    }
    // Method to convert the string to uppercase
    public function toUpperCase()
    {
        return strtoupper($this->string);
    }
```

```php
    // Method to convert the string to lowercase
    public function toLowerCase()
{

        return strtolower($this->string);

    }


    // Method to reverse the string
    public function reverse()
{

        return strrev($this->string);

    }


    // Method to get the length of the string
    public function length()
{

        return strlen($this->string);

    }


    // Method to replace a substring with another
    public function replace($search, $replace)
{

        return str_replace($search, $replace, $this->string);

    }


    // Method to return the current string
    public function getString()
{

        return $this->string;

    }


    // Method to set a new string
    public function setString($string)
{

        $this->string = $string;

    }
}
// Example usage
$manipulator = new StringManipulator("Hello, World!");

echo $manipulator->toUpperCase() . "\n"; // Outputs: HELLO, WORLD!
echo $manipulator->toLowerCase() . "\n"; // Outputs: hello, world!
```

```php
echo $manipulator->reverse() . "\n";          // Outputs: !dlroW ,olleH
echo $manipulator->length() . "\n";           // Outputs: 13
echo $manipulator->replace("World", "PHP") . "\n"; // Outputs: Hello, PHP!


// Getting and setting the string
echo $manipulator->getString() . "\n";         // Outputs: Hello, World!
$manipulator->setString("New String");
echo $manipulator->getString() . "\n";         // Outputs: New String
?>
```

5.5   Date and Time Functions

In PHP, date and time functions are essential tools that enable developers to create, manipulate, format, and display dates and times. These functions are fundamental for a wide range of applications, from simple tasks like displaying the current date to more complex operations such as scheduling events or logging timestamps.

Here's an overview of some commonly used date and time functions in PHP:

5.5.1   Date
date() is used to format a date and/or time according to a specified format.

```php
Syntax: date(string $format, int $timestamp = time())
```

Example:

```php
echo date("Y-m-d H:i:s"); // Outputs current date and time, e.g.,
2024-08-23 12:45:30
```

Parameter	Description
Format	Required. Specifies the format of the timestamp
timestamp	Optional. Specifies a timestamp. Default is the current date and time

5.5.2   Get Date:

getdate() Returns an associative array with information about the date.

```
Syntax: getdate(int $timestamp = time())
```

Example:

```
$dateInfo = getdate();
print_r($dateInfo);
```

This will return an array with keys like seconds, minutes, hours, mday, mon, year, etc.

5.5.3   Program:

demonstrates different ways to format the current date using the date() function.

```php
<?php
echo "Today is ", date("Y/m/d"), "<br>";
echo "Today is ", date("Y.m.d"), "<br>";
echo "Today is ", date("Y-m-d"), "<br>";
?>
```

5.5.4   Get the Current Time:

```php
echo date("H:i:s");
```

- **H** - Two-digit hour in 24-hour format (e.g., 00 to 23)
- h- Two-digit hour in 12-hour format (e.g., 01 to 12)
- **i** - Two-digit minutes (e.g., 00 to 59)
- **s** - Two-digit seconds (e.g., 00 to 59)
- a - Lowercase Ante meridiem and Post meridiem (am or pm   )

Program 5.5.4: get the current time

```php
<?php
echo date("h:i:s a") . "<br>"; // Outputs: 02:35:45 pm
echo date("H:i") . "<br>";     // Outputs: 14:35
echo date("h:i A") . "<br>";   // Outputs: 02:35 PM
?>
```

5.5.5   Get the Full Date and Time:

```php
echo date("Y-m-d H:i:s");
```

- **Y-m-d** - Date
- **H:i:s** – Time

Program 5.5.5: Get the Full Date and Time

```php
<?php
echo date("Y-m-d H:i:s");
?>
```

5.5.6   Get the Day of the Week:

```php
echo date("l");
```

- **l** (lowercase 'L') - Full textual representation of the day of the week

5.5.7   Get a Custom Date Format:
echo date("D, d M Y");

- **D** - Three-letter day of the week (e.g., Fri)
- **d** - Day of the month (e.g., 16)
- **M** - Three-letter month (e.g., Aug)
- **Y** - Four-digit year (e.g., 2024)

Program 5.5.7: Date and time example

```php
<?php
// Get the current day of the week
$dayOfWeek = date("l"); // Full textual representation of the day
$currentDate = date("Y-m-d"); // Full numeric representation of the date
$currentTime = date("h:i:sa"); // 12-hour format with lowercase am/pm


echo "Today is " . $dayOfWeek . "<br>";
echo "Current date is " . $currentDate . "<br>";
echo "Current time is " . $currentTime . "<br>";
?>
```

WORKING WITH COOKIES AND USER SESSIONS

Introduction

Cookies and user sessions are critical components in PHP that enable web applications to maintain state and enhance user experience across multiple requests. Both mechanisms facilitate the storage and retrieval of user-specific data, but they do so in different ways, each serving unique purposes in web development.

Cookies

Cookies are small pieces of data stored on the client's browser. When a server sends a cookie to the browser, it can be retained and sent back to the server with subsequent requests. This allows web applications to remember user preferences, authentication status, and other relevant information. Cookies are particularly useful for persisting data across different browsing sessions, enabling features like "Remember Me" functionality and tracking user behavior for analytics.

PHP provides straightforward functions for setting, retrieving, and deleting cookies, allowing developers to easily manage user data. However, developers must consider security implications, such as data sensitivity and user privacy, when implementing cookies.

User Sessions

While cookies are stored on the client side, user sessions provide a more secure way to store data on the server. A session allows developers to store user-specific information temporarily, associated with a unique session ID. This ID is typically sent to the client as a cookie or through URL parameters. Sessions are ideal for managing user authentication, as they keep sensitive data like user IDs and authentication tokens secure and out of the client's reach.

Sessions are particularly advantageous for storing temporary information that is relevant only for the duration of a user's visit, such as items in a shopping cart or user preferences for the current session.

6.1   Cookies:

Cookies are small pieces of data stored on the client's browser and they are created on the server side. They play a crucial role in maintaining stateful information across different pages of a web application.

A cookie is a key-value pair sent from a server to a client's browser and stored locally. Every time the client makes a request to the server, the browser automatically sends the stored cookies along with the request, allowing the server to recognize the user and maintain stateful interactions.

In PHP, cookies are often used to store user preferences, session data, authentication tokens, and other information that needs to persist between page reloads or visits.

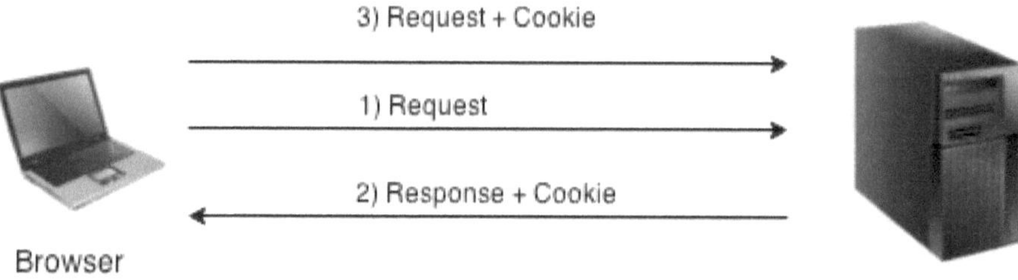

Key Characteristics of Cookies:

- **Name: The name of the cookie (key) that identifies it.**
- **Value: The data associated with the cookie, which is stored as a string.**
- **Expiration: The time after which the cookie will be deleted from the client's browser.**
- **Path: The URL path within which the cookie is accessible.**
- **Domain: Specifies the domain that can access the cookie.**
- **Secure: A flag indicating that the cookie should only be sent over secure (HTTPS) connections.**
- **HttpOnly: A flag indicating that the cookie is accessible only via the HTTP protocol and not through client-side scripts.**

Points to be noted:

- **Creation**: Cookies are set by the server using the 'setcookie()' function.

- **Storage**: Cookies are stored on the client's browser.

- **Transmission**: Cookies are sent with each HTTP request from the client to the server, where they can be accessed using the '$_COOKIE' superglobal array.

6.2 Setting a Cookie with PHP:
6.2.1 setcookie() function:

Cookies are set in PHP using the setcookie() function. This function must be called before any output is sent to the browser, as cookies are sent as HTTP headers. The 'setcookie()' function i can be used with just the name, value, and expiration time parameters to create a basic cookie.

```
Synatax: setcookie(name, value, expire);
```

Parameter	Purpose
Name	The name of the cookie.
Value	The value of the cookie.
Expire	The expiration time of the cookie in seconds.

6.2.2 Retrieving Cookies:

The $_COOKIE superglobal array is used to retrieve cookie values sent by the client browser. This array contains all the cookies that were sent to the server with the current HTTP request.

```
Syntax: $variable = $_COOKIE["CookieName"];
```

Example:

```php
if(isset($_COOKIE['user']))
{
    echo "User is: " . $_COOKIE['user']; // Outputs: User is: John Doe
} else
{
    echo "User cookie is not set.";
}
```

This code checks if the user cookie is set and, if so, retrieves and displays its value.

Points to be noted:

- **$_COOKIE["CookieName"]**: Accesses the value of the cookie with the name "CookieName".

- **$variable**: Stores the value retrieved from $_COOKIE.

Program 6.1: Demonstrates Setting and Managing Cookies in PHP

```php
<?php
$cname = "person";
$cvalue = "rayna";
// Set the cookie with the name $cname and value $cvalue
setcookie($cname, $cvalue, time() + 3600); // Cookie expires in 1 hour
?>
<!DOCTYPE html>
<html>
<body>
<?php
// Check if the cookie is set
if (!isset($_COOKIE[$cname]))
{
    echo "Cookie named " . $cname . " is not set";
}
 else
{
    echo "Cookie named " . $cname . " is set<br>";
    echo "Value is: " . $_COOKIE[$cname];
}
?>
</body>
</html>
```

6.3   Modifying a Cookie Value in PHP:

To modify the value of an existing cookie, you need to use the **setcookie**() function. This function sets a new value for the cookie by specifying its name, value, and other optional parameters. The browser will overwrite the existing cookie with the new value.

Steps to Modify a Cookie Value

1. **Set the Original Cookie**: First, you need to have a cookie already set with a certain value.

2. **Modify the Cookie Value**: To modify the cookie, simply set the cookie again with the same name but a different value.

3. **Ensure Expiry and Path are the Same**: When modifying a cookie, ensure the expiration time and path match those of the original cookie, unless you intend to change these as well.

Program 6.3: Modifying a Cookie Value in PHP

```php
<?php
// Define the cookie name
$cookie_name = 'user';
// Check if we need to update the cookie
if (isset($_GET['update']))
{
    // Set the new value for the cookie
    $new_value = 'updated_value';
     setcookie($cookie_name, $new_value, time() + 3600, '/'); //
Cookie expires in 1 hour
    echo 'Cookie value has been updated to: ' . $new_value;
} else
{
    // Set the initial value for the cookie
    $initial_value = 'initial_value';
    setcookie($cookie_name, $initial_value, time() + 3600, '/'); //
Cookie expires in 1 hour
    echo 'Initial cookie value is set to: ' . $initial_value;
}
?>
<html>
<body>
    <a href="?update=true">Update Cookie Value</a>
</body>
</html>
```

6.4 Deleting a Cookie:

To delete a cookie in PHP, you can use the 'setcookie()' function with an expiration time in the past. This effectively removes the cookie from the user's browser. Here's a step-by-step guide on how to delete a cookie:

Steps to Delete a Cookie

1. **Set the Cookie with an Expired Date**: Use setcookie() with the same name as the cookie you want to delete and set the expires parameter to a time in the past.

2. **Path and Domain**: Ensure that the path and domain parameters match those used when the cookie was originally set. This ensures that the correct cookie is deleted.

Program 6.4: Program for Deleting a Cookie

```php
<?php
$cookie_name = 'person';

// Check if we need to delete the cookie
if (isset($_GET['delete']))
{
    setcookie($cookie_name, '', time() - 3600, '/');
    header("Location: " . $_SERVER['PHP_SELF']);
    exit();
}


// Check if we need to set the cookie
if (isset($_POST['set_cookie']))
{
    $cookie_value = $_POST['cookie_value'];
    setcookie($cookie_name, $cookie_value, time() + 3600, '/'); //
Expires in 1 hour
    header("Location: " . $_SERVER['PHP_SELF']);
    exit();
}
?>
<html>
<body>
```

```php
<?php
if (!isset($_COOKIE[$cookie_name]))
{
    echo "Cookie '{$cookie_name}' is not set.";
} else
{
        echo "Cookie '{$cookie_name}' is set with value: " .
htmlspecialchars($_COOKIE[$cookie_name]);
}
?>
<br>
<!-- Form to set the cookie value -->
<form method="post">
    <label for="cookie_value">Set Cookie Value:</label>
    <input type="text" id="cookie_value" name="cookie_value">
    <button type="submit" name="set_cookie">Set Cookie</button>
</form>
<br>
<!-- Link to delete the cookie -->
<a href="?delete=true">Delete Cookie</a>
</body>
</html>
```

Checking If the Cookie Is Deleted

To verify that the cookie has been deleted, you can check if the cookie is still set in the $_COOKIE superglobal array.

```php
<?php
$cookie_name = 'person';

// Check if we need to delete the cookie
if (isset($_GET['delete']))
{
    setcookie($cookie_name, '', time() - 3600, '/');
    header("Location: " . $_SERVER['PHP_SELF'] . "?deleted=true");
// Add a query parameter for feedback
    exit();
}
```

```php
// Check if we need to set the cookie
if (isset($_POST['set_cookie']))
{
    $cookie_value = $_POST['cookie_value'];
    setcookie($cookie_name, $cookie_value, time() + 3600, '/'); //
Expires in 1 hour
    header("Location: " . $_SERVER['PHP_SELF'] . "?set=true"); //
Add a query parameter for feedback
    exit();
}
?>
<html>
<body>
<?php
// Display cookie status
if (!isset($_COOKIE[$cookie_name]))
{
    echo "Cookie '{$cookie_name}' is not set.";
} else
{
        echo "Cookie '{$cookie_name}' is set with value: " .
htmlspecialchars($_COOKIE[$cookie_name]);
}

// Check for feedback messages
if (isset($_GET['deleted']))
{
    echo "<br>Cookie '{$cookie_name}' has been deleted.";
} elseif (isset($_GET['set']))
{
    echo "<br>Cookie '{$cookie_name}' has been set.";
}
?>
<br>
<!-- Form to set the cookie value -->
<form method="post">
    <label for="cookie_value">Set Cookie Value:</label>
    <input type="text" id="cookie_value" name="cookie_value">
    <button type="submit" name="set_cookie">Set Cookie</button>
</form>
<br>
<!-- Link to delete the cookie -->
<a href="?delete=true">Delete Cookie</a>
</body>
</html>
```

6.5   Sessions in PHP

Sessions in PHP are a mechanism to store user-specific data across multiple web pages, allowing for a persistent state between requests. Unlike cookies, which are stored on the client's browser, session data is stored on the server, making it a more secure and reliable way to maintain state.

How sessions work?

When a session is started, PHP generates a unique session ID for each user. This ID is usually stored in a cookie on the client's browser. Every time the user makes a request to the server, the session ID is sent along with the request, allowing PHP to associate the request with the correct session data.

Key Features of PHP Sessions

- **State Persistence**: Sessions allow data to persist across multiple requests, enabling functionalities like user authentication, shopping carts, and user preferences.
- **Server-Side Storage**: Since session data is stored on the server, it's more secure than cookies, which are stored on the client's machine and can be easily manipulated.
- **Automatic Management**: PHP automatically manages session creation, tracking, and expiration, simplifying state management in web applications.

Sessions in PHP provide a secure, server-side method for maintaining user state across multiple pages. They are essential for building dynamic, user-driven web applications that require persistent data throughout a user's interaction with a site.

6.5.1   Starting a PHP Session

To start a session in PHP, you use the 'session_start()' function. This function initializes a session or resumes the current one based on the session identifier passed through a request (usually via a cookie). The session_start() function must be called at the very beginning of your script, before any HTML or other output is sent to the browser.

Steps to Start a Session

1. **Call session_start()**: Place this at the top of your PHP script to start or resume a session.

2. **Store Data in the Session**: Once the session is started, you can store data in the $_SESSION superglobal array.

3. **Access Session Data**: You can access and manipulate session data throughout the session's lifetime.

Example:

1. **Starting the Session**

```php
<?php
// Start the session
session_start();
?>
```

This code starts a session. If a session already exists, it resumes that session; otherwise, it creates a new session and assigns a unique session ID.

2. **Storing Data in the Session**

```php
<?php
// Start the session
session_start();

// Store data in the session
$_SESSION['username'] = 'JohnDoe';
$_SESSION['email'] = 'john.doe@example.com';
?>
```

In this example, we store the username and email of a user in the session. This data will be available across different pages for the duration of the session.

3.   **Accessing Session Data**

```php
<?php
// Start the session
session_start();
// Access session data
echo 'Username: ' . $_SESSION['username']; // Outputs: Username: JohnDoe
echo 'Email: ' . $_SESSION['email']; // Outputs: Email: john.doe@
example.com
?>
```

You can access the session data stored earlier by referencing the $_SESSION array.

Program 6.5: Setting and Accessing Session Variables in PHP

```php
<?php
// Start the session at the beginning of the script
session_start();
// Set session variables
$_SESSION['username'] = 'rayna';
$_SESSION['email'] = 'rayna@example.com';
// Retrieve and display session variables
echo 'Username: ' . $_SESSION['username'] . '<br>';
echo 'Email: ' . $_SESSION['email'];
?>
```


6.6   working with session variables:

Retrieving PHP session variable values on another webpage is a straightforward process. Once a session is started and a variable is stored in the session on one page, it can be accessed on any other page of your website, as long as the session is active.

In PHP, session variables can be accessed across different pages once they are set. This allows to retain user-specific information as the user navigates through website. To retrieve session variable values on another webpage, you must start the session on that page using the session_start() function, and then you can access the session variables using the $_SESSION superglobal array.

Steps to Retrieve PHP Session Variable Values on Another Webpage

1. **Start the Session**: On the second webpage (or any subsequent webpage where you want to access the session variables), you need to call session_start() at the beginning of your script. This ensures that the session is resumed, and the session variables are available.

2. **Access the Session Variables**: After starting the session, you can access any session variable that was previously set using the $_SESSION superglobal array.

Program 6.6: Setting and Retrieving Session Variables
Setting Session Variables (set_session.php):

```php
<?php
// Start the session
session_start();
// Set session variables
$_SESSION["a"] = "blue";    // Favorite color
$_SESSION["b"] = "dog";     // Favorite animal
?>
<a href="get_session.php">Go to Get Session Page</a>
```

Retrieving Session Variables (get_session.php):
To retrieve and display the session variables, you can use this script:

```php
<?php
// Start the session
session_start();
// Check if session variables are set
if (isset($_SESSION["a"]) && isset($_SESSION["b"]))
{
    echo "Favorite color is " . $_SESSION["a"] . "<br>";
    echo "Favorite animal is " . $_SESSION["b"];
} else
{
    echo "Session variables are not set.";
}
?>
<a href="set_session.php">Go back to Set Session Page</a>
```

Explanation

1. **set_session.php**:

   ○ **Session Initialization**: session_start(); is called to start or resume the session.

   ○ **Setting Variables**: Session variables $_SESSION["a"] and $_SESSION["b"] are set with values "blue" and "dog", respectively.

   ○ **Navigation**: The HTML link navigates to get_session.php, where the session variables will be displayed.

2. **get_session.php**:

   ○ **Session Initialization**: session_start(); is called to access the existing session.

   ○ **Accessing Variables**: It checks if the session variables are set and displays their values. If not, it shows a message indicating that the variables are not set.

   ○ **Navigation**: The HTML link allows returning to the set_session.php page.

6.7 Modifying a PHP Session Variable

To modify a session variable in PHP, you simply overwrite its existing value by assigning a new value to it. When you need to update the value of a session variable, you can do so by directly assigning a new value to it. The $_SESSION superglobal array is used to manage session variables. Once a session is started with session_start(), you can update any session variable by reassigning it.

Program 6.7: Modifying a PHP Session Variable

```php
<?php
// Start the session at the beginning of the script
session_start();

// Set initial session variables
$_SESSION['username'] = 'rayna';
$_SESSION['email'] = 'rayna@example.com';

// Display initial session variables
echo 'Initial Username: ' . $_SESSION['username'] . '<br>';
echo 'Initial Email: ' . $_SESSION['email'] . '<br>';

// Modify session variables
$_SESSION['username'] = 'rachel';
$_SESSION['email'] = 'rachel@example.com';

// Display updated session variables
echo 'Updated Username: ' . $_SESSION['username'] . '<br>';
echo 'Updated Email: ' . $_SESSION['email'];
?>
```

6.8   Destroying a PHP Session:

To completely remove all session variables and destroy a PHP session, you need to use both session_unset() and session_destroy() functions. Here's how each function works and how to use them together:

1. **session_unset()**: This function clears all session variables. It removes all data associated with the current session but does not destroy the session itself.

2. **session_destroy()**: This function destroys the session data on the server. After calling this function, the session is no longer valid, and the session ID is deleted.

Steps to Destroy a Session:

1. **Call session_start()**: Begin by starting the session to ensure that you can access session variables and the session data.

2.   **Call session_unset()**: This will clear all the session variables.

3.   **Call session_destroy()**: This will destroy the session data on the server.

Example Code

```php
<?php
// Start the session
session_start();

// Display current session variables
echo 'Username: ' . (isset($_SESSION['username']) ? $_
SESSION['username']: 'Not set') . '<br>';
echo 'Email: ' . (isset($_SESSION['email']) ? $_SESSION['email']:
'Not set') . '<br>';

// Unset all session variables
session_unset();

// Destroy the session
session_destroy();

// Optionally, delete the session cookie
if (ini_get("session.use_cookies"))
{
    $params = session_get_cookie_params();
    setcookie(session_name(), '', time() - 42000,
        $params["path"], $params["domain"],
        $params["secure"], $params["httponly"]
    );
}

// Verify that the session is destroyed
session_start(); // Restart the session to check
if (!isset($_SESSION['username']) && !isset($_SESSION['email']))
{
    echo 'Session has been destroyed and all session variables
removed.';
} else
{
    echo 'Session variables are still set.';
}
?>
```

In summary, cookies and user sessions in PHP are essential for creating dynamic, interactive web applications. Understanding how to effectively implement and manage both mechanisms enables developers to enhance user experience, maintain state across requests, and ensure secure data handling. Together, they form a powerful toolkit for building robust web applications that cater to the needs of users while adhering to best practices in security and privacy.

WORKING WITH FILES AND IMAGES

Introduction

In the dynamic landscape of web development, handling files and images is a crucial aspect of creating interactive and visually appealing applications. PHP provides robust capabilities for managing various file types, allowing developers to read, write, upload, and manipulate files seamlessly. Whether you're building a content management system, an e-commerce platform, or a user-driven website, understanding how to work with files in PHP is essential.

Images are a fundamental component of web design and user experience, enhancing the visual appeal of websites and applications. In PHP, handling images effectively allows developers to manipulate, optimize, and display images dynamically, catering to user needs and improving engagement. Whether you are building a photo gallery, an e-commerce platform, or an online portfolio, understanding how to work with images in PHP is essential for creating interactive and visually compelling applications.

The Importance of File Handling

File handling in PHP enables you to manage user-generated content, store data, and integrate multimedia elements into your applications. Common scenarios include:

- **Uploading User Files**: Allowing users to upload documents, images, or other files to your server for storage or processing.

- **Generating Dynamic Content**: Creating files dynamically, such as PDFs, text files, or images, based on user interactions or data stored in a database.

- **Reading and Writing Data**: Managing data files (like CSV or JSON) for importing or exporting information between your application and external systems.

The Importance of Image Handling

Image handling in PHP enables you to perform a variety of operations, including uploading, resizing, cropping, and manipulating images programmatically. Common scenarios where image handling is crucial include:

- **User-Uploaded Images**: Allowing users to upload their photos or graphics for profile pictures, product images, or content submissions.

- **Dynamic Image Generation**: Creating images on-the-fly based on user input or data from a database, such as generating charts or customized graphics.

- **Image Optimization**: Reducing file sizes to improve website performance and loading times without compromising quality.

Real-World Applications of Files and Images in PHP

1. **User Profile Management**: Websites allow users to upload profile pictures, which enhances personalization and engagement.

2. **Backup Solutions**: PHP scripts can be utilized to create backup files of databases or application data, enabling data recovery and redundancy.

3. **Form Submissions with File Uploads**: Many web applications incorporate file upload fields in forms, such as submitting documents for job applications or uploading assignments in educational platforms.

4. **File Sharing Applications**: Applications like Google Drive or Dropbox use PHP for file uploads, downloads, and management, allowing users to share documents and files securely.

5. **E-commerce Product Images**: Online stores enable merchants to upload product images, which are displayed on product pages to enhance the shopping experience.

6. **Content Management Systems (CMS)**: Platforms like WordPress and Joomla use PHP for managing images uploaded by users, allowing for easy integration into posts and pages.

7. **Image Uploads for Social Media**: Social networking sites allow users to share images, using PHP to handle uploads and optimize images for display.

8. **Image Processing and Resizing**: Applications that require image editing or processing, such as cropping or adding filters, often use PHP libraries like GD or ImageMagick.

7.1   Including Files with include()

The 'include' statement in PHP imports all the content from the specified file and inserts it into the current file at the location of the include statement. This functionality allows developers to reuse common elements, such as headers, footers, or navigation menus, across multiple pages of a website, promoting code modularity and reducing redundancy.

Syntax:

```
include 'filename.php';
```

Key points:

- **include**: The keyword that tells PHP to insert the content of another file into the current script.
- **'filename.php'**: The path to the file you want to include. This can be a relative path (e.g., 'header.php') or an absolute path (e.g., '/var/www/html/header.php').

Program 7.1: Including Files with include()

Suppose you have a file called *header.php* that contains your website's header code:

```
<!DOCTYPE html>
<html>
<head>
    <title>My Website</title>
</head>
<body>
    <header>
        <h1>Welcome to My Website</h1>
    </header>
```

Now, you can include this header in any other PHP file called "index.php" as given below,

```
<?php include 'header.php'; ?>
<main>
    <p>This is the main content of the page.</p>
</main>
<footer>
    <p> 2024 My Website</p>
</footer>
</body>
</html>
```

7.2   Creating, Deleting, and Closing Files

7.2.1   Creating Files:

The fopen() function is used to create or open files in PHP. It requires two parameters: the name of the file and the mode in which you want to open it (e.g., for reading, writing, etc.).

Syntax:

```
$filePointer = fopen("filename", "mode");
```

Parameters:

- **"filename"**: The name of the file to open. This can be a relative or absolute path.
- **"mode"**: The mode in which to open the file, Commonly include:
- **"r"**: Read-only. Opens the file for reading. The file pointer is placed at the beginning of the file.
- **"w"**: Write-only. Opens the file for writing. If the file exists, it truncates (clears) the file to zero length. If the file does not exist, it creates a new file.

- **"a"**: Write-only. Opens the file for writing. If the file exists, the file pointer is placed at the end of the file. If the file does not exist, it creates a new file. The new data will be written at the end of the file (appended).

Program 7.2.1: Creating a file

```
<?
$filename = "newfile.txt";
$filePointer = fopen($filename, "w");
if ($filePointer)
{
    fwrite($filePointer, "This is a new file created with PHP.");
    fclose($filePointer);
    echo "File '$filename' created successfully.";
} else
{
    echo "Error: Unable to create the file '$filename'.";
}
?>
```

7.2.2 Deleting Files:

The unlink() function is used to delete a file in PHP. This function permanently removes a specified file from the file system. It is commonly used when you need to delete files that are no longer needed, such as temporary files, uploaded files, or files generated dynamically by the application. Before deleting a file, it is good practice to check if the file exists to avoid errors.

Syntax:

```
unlink("filename");
```

Parameters:

- **filename"**: The name of the file you want to delete. This can be a relative or absolute path.

Program 7.2.2: Program for deleting a file

```php
<?php
$filename = "sample.txt";
if (file_exists($filename))
{
    if (unlink($filename))
    {
        echo "The file '$filename' was deleted successfully.";
    } else
    {
        echo "Error: Unable to delete the file '$filename'.";
    }

} else
{
    echo "Error: File '$filename' does not exist.";
}
?>
```

7.2.3   Closing Files:

After working with a file, it is important to close it. This step frees up system resources and ensures that all data is saved properly. closing a file is done using the fclose() function. This function is used to close an open file pointer, freeing up system resources associated with the file. Closing a file is an important step after performing file operations such as reading or writing, as it ensures that all data is properly written and that the file is no longer locked or held open by the script.

Syntax:

```php
fclose($filePointer);
```

parameters:

```php
$filePointer: The file pointer resource returned by fopen().
```

Program 7.2.3: Program for closing a file

```php
<?php
$filePointer = fopen("example.txt", "w");
if ($filePointer)
{
    fwrite($filePointer, "Hello, world!");
    fclose($filePointer); // Closes the file
    echo "File operations completed and file closed.";
} else
{
    echo "Error: Unable to open the file.";
}
?>
```

Explanation:

- **fopen("example.txt", "w"):** Opens example.txt for writing and returns a file pointer.

- **fwrite($filePointer, "Hello, world!"):** Writes data to the file.

- **fclose($filePointer):** Closes the file pointer, which is crucial for freeing up system resources and ensuring that all data is written to the file.

Always ensure you close files after completing operations to maintain good resource management and avoid potential issues.

7.3   Reading Data from Files in PHP

Reading from files is a fundamental operation in PHP that allows you to access and manipulate the contents of a file. This can be done using various functions that cater to different needs, such as reading a file line by line or reading the entire file content at once.

Opening a File

To read data from a file, you first need to open it using the fopen() function. This function requires two arguments: the name of the file and the mode in which you want to open it.

Example:

```
$filename = "example.txt";
$file = fopen($filename, "r"); // "r" stands for read-only mode
```

Reading from a File

Once the file is opened, there are several functions can be used to read the data,

1. **fread()**: Reads a specified number of bytes from the file.

2. **fgets()**: Reads a line from the file.

3. **fgetcsv()**: Reads a line from a CSV file and parses it into an array.

4. **file_get_contents()**: Reads the entire file into a string.

7.3.1   fread()

The fread() function reads a specified number of bytes from a file. This is useful for reading a specific amount of data from a file, which can be beneficial when dealing with binary files or when you need to read a chunk of data.

Syntax:

```
$data = fread($fileHandle, $length);
```

Parameters:

*   **$fileHandle:** A file handle (file pointer) resource that is typically created by fopen().

*   **$length:** The number of bytes to read from the file.

Working of fread()

*   fread() reads up to $length bytes from the file pointer referred to by $handle.

*   If the file pointer is at the end of the file (EOF), fread() will return false.

*   The actual number of bytes read may be less than $length if fread() encounters an end-of-file (EOF) or if it is interrupted by a signal.

Program 7.3.2: Reading Data from Files

```php
<?php
$filename = "example.txt";
$file = fopen($filename, "r");
if ($file)
{
    // Read the first 100 bytes from the file
    $content = fread($file, 100);
    echo $content;
    // Close the file
    fclose($file);
} else
{
    echo "Unable to open the file.";
}
?>
```

In this example:

- The file example.txt is opened in read-only mode ("r").
- fread() reads 100 bytes from the file and stores it in the $content variable.
- The content is then printed out.
- The file is closed using fclose().

Reading a File in Chunks

When dealing with large files, you might want to read the file in smaller chunks to avoid high memory usage.

```php
<?php
$filename = "largefile.txt";
$file = fopen($filename, "r");
if ($file)
{
    while (!feof($file))
    {
        $chunk = fread($file, 8192); // Read 8KB at a time
        echo $chunk;
    }
    fclose($file);
} else
{
    echo "Unable to open the file.";
}
?>
```

In this example, the file is read in 8KB chunks until the end of the file is reached (feof($file) returns true).

Error Handling

It's important to handle errors when using fread():

- Always check if the file was successfully opened before attempting to read.
- Be aware that fread() might return fewer bytes than requested if it reaches the end of the file or if an error occurs.

Example with Error Handling:

```php
<?php
$filename = "example.txt";
$file = fopen($filename, "r");
if ($file)
{
    $content = fread($file, 100);
    if ($content === false)
    {
        echo "Error reading file.";
    } else
    {
        echo $content;
    }
    fclose($file);
} else
{
    echo "Unable to open the file.";
}
?>
```

7.3.2   fgets()

The fgets() function in PHP is used to read a single line from an open file. It reads up to a specified number of bytes or until it encounters a newline character, whichever comes first. This is useful for processing files line by line, such as when reading text files where each line represents a distinct piece of data.

Syntax:

```php
$line = fgets($fileHandle, $length);
```

Parameters:

- **$handle:** A file handle resource that is typically created by fopen().

- **$length (optional):** The maximum number of bytes to read. If not specified, fgets() will read until it reaches the end of the line (\n), the end of the file, or the maximum buffer size (typically 1024 bytes).

Working of fgets()

- fgets() reads a line from the file and moves the file pointer to the start of the next line.

- If the length parameter is set, it will read up to that many bytes or until it encounters a newline character (\n), whichever comes first.

- If the end of the file is reached (EOF), fgets() will return false.

Program 7.3.1: Reading Data from Files Using fgets()

```php
<?php
$filename = "example.txt";
$file = fopen($filename, "r");
if ($file)
{
    while (($line = fgets($file)) !== false)
{
        echo $line . "<br>";
    }
    fclose($file);
} else
{
    echo "Unable to open the file.";
}
?>
```

In this example:

- The file example.txt is opened in read-only mode ("r").

- The fgets() function is used inside a while loop to read each line of the file until the end is reached.

    Each line is printed with a line break (<br>) for display in a web context.

- The file is closed using fclose().

Reading a Limited Number of Characters

You can specify the maximum number of characters to read by passing the parameter:

```php
<?php
$filename = "example.txt";
$file = fopen($filename, "r");
if ($file)
{
    $line = fgets($file, 50); // Read up to 50 characters or until the end of the line
    echo $line;
    fclose($file);
} else
{
    echo "Unable to open the file.";
}
?>
```

In this example, fgets() will read up to 50 characters from the first line, or stop earlier if it encounters a newline.

Error Handling

It's important to handle errors when using fgets():

- Always check if the file was successfully opened before attempting to read.

- Be prepared to handle cases where fgets() returns false, indicating the end of the file or an error.

Example with Error Handling:

```php
<?php
$filename = "example.txt";
$file = fopen($filename, "r");
if ($file)
{
    while (($line = fgets($file)) !== false)
    {
        echo $line . "<br>";
    }
    if (!feof($file))
    {
        echo "Error: unexpected fgets() fail\n";
    }
```

```
    fclose($file);
} else
{
    echo "Unable to open the file.";
}
?>
```

In this example, after reading the file line by line, the feof() function is used to check if the end of the file was reached. If not, it indicates an error occurred during reading.

7.3.3   file_get_contents()

This PHP function reads the entire contents of a file into a string. It takes the file path as its parameter and returns the file's contents. If the file cannot be read, it returns false. This function is useful for quickly loading the contents of a file into a variable for processing. It's a simple and efficient way to get the content of a file, and is often used for tasks like reading text files, HTML files.

Syntax:

```
$content = file_get_contents("filename");
```

Parameters:

- **filename:** Name of the file.

Program 7.3.1: Reading Data from Files Using file_get_contents()

```php
<?php
// Reading a local file
$content = file_get_contents("example.txt");
echo $content;
// Reading a remote file (e.g., a web page)
$webContent = file_get_contents("https://example.com");
echo $webContent;
?>
```

7.4   Writing to Files

In PHP, you can write new data to files or append data to existing files using specific file modes with the fopen() function.

Writing to files in PHP allows you to store data persistently, such as saving user input, logs, or dynamically generated content.PHP provides various functions for file handling, with file_put_contents() being a simple way to write data to a file in one step. For more control over the process, fopen() and fwrite() allow you to open files, write data, and manage files with different modes, such as writing or appending. Proper file handling includes managing permissions and ensuring the file is successfully opened before writing.

7.4.1   Using fwrite():

The fwrite() function is used to write data to a file that has been opened with fopen(). This function gives you more control over the file writing process.

Syntax:

```
fwrite($fileHandle, $data);
```

Parameters:

- **$fileHandle:** The file pointer resource, obtained from fopen().
- **$data:** The data to be written to the file.

Steps:
Open the file using fopen().

```
Write data to the file using fwrite().
```

Close the file using fclose().

```
Program 7.4.1 (a): Writing to a File Using fwrite()
<?php
// Open the file for writing (w)
$file = fopen("example.txt", "w");
// Write some content
$txt = "This is a new line of text.";
fwrite($file, $txt);
// Close the file
fclose($file);
?>
```

7.4.2   Using fputs()

The fputs() function writes data to a file, just like fwrite(). It is provided for compatibility with older PHP code and can be used interchangeably with fwrite().

Syntax:

```
fputs($fileHandle, $data);
```

Parameters:

- **$fileHandle:** The file pointer resource, obtained from fopen().

- **$data:** The data to be written to the file.

Program 7.4.2: Writing to a File Using fputs()

```
<?php
$fileHandle = fopen("example.txt", "w");
$data = "This is some text written with fputs().";
fputs($fileHandle, $data);
fclose($fileHandle);
?>
```

7.4.3   Handling Errors

It's important to handle errors when working with files, such as checking if the file was opened successfully.

Program 7.4.2: Handling Errors

```php
<?php
$file = fopen("example.txt", "w");
if ($file)
{
    fwrite($file, "Hello, error handling!");
    fclose($file);
} else
{
    echo "Failed to open the file!";
}
?>
```

7.5   Appending to a File

Appending to files in PHP allows you to add new data to the end of an existing file without affecting overwriting its content. This is commonly used for log files, where each new entry is added after the previous ones. Use fopen() with the "a" mode (append) along with fwrite() for more control. Appending ensures that the original content of the file remains intact while new data is added.

Syntax:

```php
$fileHandle = fopen("filename", "a");
```

For more control over the file-handling process, you can use fopen() to open the file in append mode ("a"), and then use fwrite() to append the content.

Steps:

1.   Open the file in append mode ("a").

2.   Write the new data to the file.

3.   Close the file to ensure the changes are saved.

Program 7.5: Appending to a File

```php
<?php
// Open the file in append mode
$fileHandle = fopen("example.txt", "a");
if ($fileHandle)
{
    // Write data to the file
    $txt = "Appending this line of text.\n"; // Added a newline for
better formatting
    fwrite($fileHandle, $txt);
    // Close the file
    fclose($fileHandle); // Fixed the variable name here
} else
{
    echo "Failed to open the file!";
}
?>
```

7.6   Working with Directories

Working with directories in PHP allows you to manage and manipulate folders on the server, such as creating, deleting, reading, and navigating through directories. PHP provides functions like mkdir() for creating directories, rmdir() for removing them, and opendir() and readdir() for reading directory contents. Directory handling is useful for organizing files, managing uploads, or creating dynamic folder structures in applications. Proper permission handling is crucial when working with directories to ensure the script has the necessary access rights. Here's a breakdown of the essential concepts and functions for managing directories in PHP:

7.6.1   Creating Directories:

Directories can be created using the mkdir() function, which allows you to specify the name, permissions, and whether to create parent directories automatically. This function is useful when you need to dynamically generate folder structures, such as for file uploads or organizing data.

The syntax for the mkdir() function in PHP, without the optional parameters is,

Syntax:

```php
mkdir("path/to/directory");
```

This creates the directory with the default permissions (usually 0777), subject to the current umask. You can specify the mode (permissions) if needed.

```php
mkdir("path/to/directory", 0755);
```

Here, 0755 gives the owner full permissions and read/execute permissions to everyone else.

Program 7.6.1(a). creating a directory and with a specific permissions creating a directory

```php
<?php
// Create a directory named "new_folder"
if (mkdir("rayna"))
{
    echo "Directory created successfully.";
} else
{
    echo "Failed to create directory.";
}
?>
```

Program. 7.6.1(b). Creating directory with permissions

```php
// Create a directory with read/write permissions for the owner,
group, and others
<?php
if (mkdir("secure_folder", 0755))
{
    echo "Directory created with specific permissions.";
} else
{
    echo "Failed to create directory.";
}
?>
```

7.6.2 Checking If a Directory Exists:

You can check if a directory exists using the is_dir() function. This function checks whether a given path refers to an existing directory, allowing you to perform actions based on its existence, such as creating the directory if it doesn't exist or handling errors.

Syntax:

```
is_dir("path/to/directory");
```

Program simple PHP program that demonstrates how to create a directory:

Program.7.6.2(a): Basic Directory Existence Check

```php
<?php
$dir = "example_folder";
if (is_dir($dir))
{
    echo "The directory '$dir' exists.";
} else
{
    echo "The directory '$dir' does not exist.";
}
?>
```

Program.7.6.2(b): Creating a Directory if it Doesn't Exist

```php
<?php
$dir = "example_folder";
if (!is_dir($dir))
{
    if (mkdir($dir))
    {
        echo "Directory '$dir' was created.";
    } else
    {
        echo "Failed to create directory '$dir'.";
    }
} else
{
    echo "The directory '$dir' already exists.";
}
?>
```

Notes:

- **Return Value**: is_dir() returns true if the path exists and is a directory, and false otherwise.

- **Permissions**: Ensure the PHP script has the necessary permissions to access or create directories, especially when working in restricted environments.

7.6.3   Opening and Reading Directories:

Open and read directories using functions like opendir(), readdir(), and closedir(). These functions allow you to loop through the contents of a directory and process each file or folder inside it.

Key Functions:

1. opendir(): Opens a directory handle, making it ready for reading.

2. readdir(): Reads entries (files/folders) from the directory.

3. closedir(): Closes the directory handle after reading.

Syntax:

```php
$dir = opendir("path/to/directory");
while (($file = readdir($dir)) !== false)
{
    // Process $file
}
closedir($dir);
```

The readdir() function should be called in a loop to read all entries in the directory.

```php
<?php
$dir = "example_folder";   // Specify the directory name
// Open the directory
if (is_dir($dir))
{
    if ($dh = opendir($dir))
    {
```

```php
        // Loop through the directory entries
        while (($file = readdir($dh)) !== false)
    {

            echo "Filename: " . $file . "<br>";
        }
        // Close the directory handle
        closedir($dh);
    }
} else
{
    echo "The directory does not exist.";
}
?>
```

The functions involved in the above program are explained below,

- **is_dir($dir):** Checks if the specified path is a directory.

- **opendir($dir):** Opens the directory and returns a handle ($dh), which is used to read its contents.

- **readdir($dh):** Iterates through the directory's files and folders, returning each item one at a time until all entries are read.

- **closedir($dh):** Closes the directory handle once reading is complete.

7.6.4 Removing Directories:

Directories can be removed using the rmdir() function, which deletes an empty directory. If the directory contains files or other directories, you must first delete those contents before removing the directory.

Syntax:

```php
rmdir("path/to/directory");
rmdir("uploads");
```

Program.7.6.4.(a): Removing an Empty Directory

```php
<?php
$dir = "example_folder";
// Check if the directory exists and is empty
if (is_dir($dir))
{
    if (rmdir($dir))
    {
        echo "Directory '$dir' was removed.";
    } else
    {
        echo "Failed to remove directory '$dir'.";
    }
} else
{
    echo "The directory '$dir' does not exist.";
}
?>
```

Program.7.6.4(b): Removing a Directory and Its Contents

To remove a directory that contains files or subdirectories, you need to first delete the contents recursively, then remove the directory itself. You can use a custom function for this task.

```php
<?php
function deleteDir($dir)
{
    if (!is_dir($dir))
    {
        return false;
    }

    // Open the directory
    $items = scandir($dir);
    foreach ($items as $item)
    {
        if ($item === "." || $item === "..")
        {
            continue;
        }
```

```php
        $path = $dir . DIRECTORY_SEPARATOR . $item; // Use DIRECTORY_
SEPARATOR for cross-platform compatibility
        // If it's a directory, recurse into it
        if (is_dir($path))
{

            deleteDir($path);
        } else
{

            // Delete file
            unlink($path);
        }
    }
    // Remove the now-empty directory
    return rmdir($dir);
}


$dir = "C:\\xampp\\htdocs\\rayna"; // Use double backslashes for
Windows paths
if (deleteDir($dir))
{
    echo "Directory '$dir' and its contents were removed.";
} else
{
    echo "Failed to remove directory '$dir'.";
}
?>
```

7.6.5   Getting Directory Contents

To get the contents of a directory, functions like scandir(), opendir() and readdir() can be used. Each function provides different ways to retrieve and manage the files and subdirectories within a directory.

Using scandir()

The scandir() function returns an array of files and directories inside the specified directory. This is a straightforward way to get all contents.

```php
Syntax:   $files = scandir("path/to/directory");
<?php
$dir = "C:\\xampp\\df";

if (is_dir($dir))
{ // Check if the directory exists
    $contents = scandir($dir);
    foreach ($contents as $item)
{
if ($item !== "." && $item !== "..")
{ // Use strict comparison
            echo "Filename: " . htmlspecialchars($item) . "<br>";
// Use htmlspecialchars for safety
        }
    }
} else
{
    echo "Directory '$dir' does not exist.";
}
?>
```

7.7   Working with Images

Working with images in PHP involves creating, manipulating, uploading, resizing, displaying images and outputting images dynamically using the GD library. The GD library is a powerful tool in PHP that allows for creating and manipulating images of various formats, including PNG, JPEG, GIF, and others. Here's an overview of common tasks and functions when working with images in PHP.

The full form of the GD library is **"Graphics Draw"** or **"Graphic Device."** The library was originally developed by Thomas Boutell in 1994 for the purpose of creating and manipulating images in various formats. It supports various image formats, and you can use it to generate images dynamically based on user input, database content, or other data sources. The GD library is commonly used in PHP for tasks like creating dynamic images, generating charts, and handling other image-related operations.

7.7.1   Creating a New Image

To create a new image in PHP, you typically use the imagecreate() function. This function creates a blank image with a specified width and height. The imagecreate() function returns a blank image of the given size. This function is part of the GD library

Syntax:

```
imagecreate($width, $height);
```

Parameters:

- **$width:** The width of the image in pixels.
- **$height:** The height of the image in pixels.

imagecreate() creates an image with a palette of colors (an indexed image). It uses a limited set of colors, which may result in less detailed images. It is typically used when creating GIF images or when you want to use a limited color palette.

The imagecolorallocate() function in PHP is used to allocate a color to an image. This color can be used as the background color or for drawing and writing on the image. The function assigns a color based on the provided RGB (Red, Green, Blue) values.

```
Syntax: int imagecolorallocate($image, int $red, int $green, int $blue);
```

Return Value:
The function returns an integer identifier representing the allocated color. This identifier can then be used when drawing shapes, lines, text, or setting the background color of the image.

Ptogram.7.7.1 Image creation with imagecreate()

```php
<?php
// Create a blank image
$image = imagecreate(200, 100);
// Allocate a background color (white)
$background_color = imagecolorallocate($image, 255, 255, 255);
// Allocate a foreground color (blue)
$blue_color = imagecolorallocate($image, 0, 0, 255);
?>
```

In the above program, imagecreate() creates an image with a palette of colors (an indexed image). It uses a limited set of colors, which may result in less detailed images. It is typically used when creating GIF images or when you want to use a limited color palette. **However, the current code does not display the image on the screen or save it to a file.**

7.7.2 Output the image:

Key Steps to Output the Image:

1. **Set the Content-Type Header**: Use header('Content-Type: image/png') to tell the browser to expect a PNG image.

2. **Generate the Image**: The imagepng($image) function outputs the image directly to the browser.

3. **Memory Management**: Use imagedestroy($image) to free up the memory associated with the image once it's been output.

Program: 7.7.2 Image creation and displaysing the image

```php
<?php
// Create a blank image
$image = imagecreate(200, 100);
// Allocate a background color (white)
$background_color = imagecolorallocate($image, 255, 255, 255);
// Allocate a foreground color (blue)
$blue_color = imagecolorallocate($image, 0, 0, 255);
// Set the content type header
header('Content-Type: image/png');
// Output the image as PNG
imagepng($image);
imagedestroy($image)
// Free up memory
?>
```

7.7.3 imagestring():

The imagestring() function in PHP is used to draw a string (text) onto an image. This function places the specified string at a given position within the image, using a specified font and color.

Syntax:

```
bool imagestring(GdImage $image, int $font, int $x, int $y, string
$string, int $color);
```

Parameters:

- **GdImage $image**: The image resource created by functions like imagecreate() where the string will be drawn.
- **int $font**: The font size to use for the string. This can be an integer from 1 to 5, with 1 being the smallest and 5 the largest.
- **int $x**: The x-coordinate (horizontal position) where the string will start.
- **int $y**: The y-coordinate (vertical position) where the string will start.
- **string $string**: The actual string (text) that you want to insert into the image.
- **int $color**: The color identifier for the text, which is typically created with imagecolorallocate().

Return Value: Returns true on success or false on failure.

Program: 7.7.3 Print text onto an image

```php
<?php
// Create a blank image
$image = imagecreate(200, 100);
// Allocate a background color
$background_color = imagecolorallocate($image, 255, 255, 255);
// Allocate a text color
$text_color = imagecolorallocate($image, 0, 0, 0);
// Draw the string on the image
imagestring($image, 3, 50, 30, "Hello, World!", $text_color);
// Output the image to the browser
header("Content-Type: image/png");
imagepng($image);
// Free up memory
imagedestroy($image);
?>
```

In the above program, The string "Hello, World!" is drawn on the image at position (50, 30) with font size 3 and the color allocated earlier.

7.8   Drawing a New Image

Drawing a new image in PHP involves creating a blank canvas, defining colors, and then drawing shapes, lines or text on that canvas. The PHP GD library provides a powerful set of functions for creating and manipulating images. Below is an overview of the process for drawing a new image.

Step1: Creating a New Image

To begin drawing, first create a blank image using the imagecreate() function. This function allow to specify the dimensions of the canvas.

Example:

```
$image = imagecreate(400, 300); // Creates a blank image with
400x300 pixels
```

Step2: Allocating Colors

Once the image is created, need to allocate colors using the imagecolorallocate() function. This function defines the colors that will be used in the image, such as the background color, text color, and colors for shapes.

Syntax:

```
$background_color = imagecolorallocate($image, 255, 255, 255); //
White background
$border_color = imagecolorallocate($image, 0, 0, 0); // Black color
for border
$text_color = imagecolorallocate($image, 0, 0, 255); // Blue color
for text
```

Step3: Drawing Basic Shapes

Now, draw the basic shapes like lines, rectangles, ellipses, and more using the GD library functions.

Line: Draw a line using imageline().
Syntax:

```
imageline($image, 10, 10, 400, 300, $line_color);
```

Rectangle: Draw a rectangle using imagerectangle().
Syntax:

```
imagerectangle($image, 50, 50, 350, 250, $border_color);
```

Ellipse: Draw an ellipse using imageellipse().
Syntax:

```
imageellipse($image, 200, 150, 100, 50, $ellipse_color);
```

Step4: Add Text

To add text to image, use the imagestring() function, where the position, font, and color of the text specified.

Example:

```
imagestring($image, 5, 150, 120, "Hello, World!", $text_color); //
Draws text
```

Step5: Outputting the Image

After drawing the desired shapes and text, then output the image. PHP supports various formats like PNG, JPEG, and GIF. Use the appropriate function for format and set the correct content type header.

Example: Outputting as PNG:

```php
header("Content-Type: image/png");
imagepng($image);
header("Content-Type: image/png");
imagepng($image);
```

Step6: Saving the Image

Instead of outputting directly to the browser, save the image to a file.

Example: Saving as PNG:

```php
imagepng($image, "path/to/save/image.png");
```

Step7: Freeing Memory

After done with the image, it's important to free the memory associated with it using the imagedestroy() function.

```php
Syntax: imagedestroy($image);
```

Program: 7.8:Drawing a new image

```php
<?php
// Create a blank image
$image = imagecreate(400, 300);
// Allocate colors
$background_color = imagecolorallocate($image, 255, 255, 255); //
White background
$border_color = imagecolorallocate($image, 0, 0, 0); // Black border
$text_color = imagecolorallocate($image, 0, 0, 255); // Blue text
// Draw a rectangle
imagerectangle($image, 50, 50, 350, 250, $border_color);
// Add text inside the rectangle
imagestring($image, 5, 150, 150, "Hello, World!", $text_color);
// Output the image as a PNG
```

```
header("Content-Type: image/png");
imagepng($image);
// Free up memory
imagedestroy($image);
?>
```

7.9 Getting Fancy with Pie Charts:

In PHP, creating pie charts and similar graphical elements can be accomplished using the imagefilledarc() function. This function is used to draw filled arcs, which can be combined to form pie charts, circles, and other shapes.

Syntax:

```
imagefilledarc(GdImage  $image,  int  $cx,int  $cy,int  $width,int
$height,int start,int $end,int $color,int $style);
```

Parameters:

- **$image**: The image resource on which the arc will be drawn.
- **$cx**: The x-coordinate of the center of the arc.
- **$cy**: The y-coordinate of the center of the arc.
- **$width**: The width of the arc.
- **$height**: The height of the arc.
- **$start**: The starting angle of the arc, in degrees.
- **$end**: The ending angle of the arc, in degrees. Positive values are clockwise, negative are counterclockwise.
- **$color**: A color identifier created using imagecolorallocate().
- **$style**: A bitwise OR of one or more of the following style constants:

  1. IMG_ARC_PIE: Draw a filled pie slice.
  2. IMG_ARC_CHORD: Draw a chord (a straight line connecting the start and end points).
  3. IMG_ARC_NOFILL: Don't fill the arc (draw only the outline).

Program: 7.9: Drawing a Pie Chart

```php
<?php
// Create a blank image with dimensions 300x300 pixels
$img = imagecreate(300, 300);
// Allocate colors
$bg = imagecolorallocate($img, 255, 255, 255); // White background
$green = imagecolorallocate($img, 0, 255, 0); // Green color for
one pie slice
$red = imagecolorallocate($img, 255, 0, 0); // Red color for another
pie slice
$blue = imagecolorallocate($img, 0, 0, 255); // Blue color for
another pie slice
// Draw the first pie slice (from 0 to 90 degrees)
imagefilledarc($img, 150, 150, 200, 100, 0, 90, $green, IMG_ARC_
PIE);
// Draw the second pie slice (from 91 to 180 degrees)
imagefilledarc($img, 150, 150, 200, 100, 91, 180, $red, IMG_ARC_
PIE);
// Draw the third pie slice (from 181 to 360 degrees)
imagefilledarc($img, 150, 150, 200, 100, 181, 360, $blue, IMG_ARC_
PIE);
// Set the content type to PNG and output the image
header("Content-Type: image/png");
imagepng($img);
// Free up memory by destroying the image resource
imagedestroy($img);
?>
```

7.10   Modifying Existing Images

Modifying existing images in PHP involves loading an image file into memory and then making changes to it, such as drawing shapes, adding text, or applying filters.

Loading an Existing Image:

To modify an existing image, first load it using the appropriate function based on the image format. For a PNG image, use imagecreatefrompng().

Example:

```php
$image = imagecreatefrompng('C:\xampp\htdocs\rachel\mr.PNG');
```

Program 7.10: Example of Modifying an Existing Image

```php
<?php
// Load the existing PNG image
$image = imagecreatefrompng('C:\xampp\htdocs\raj\cce.PNG');
$text_color = imagecolorallocate($image, 255, 255, 0);
imagestring($image, 5, 20, 20, "Modified Image", $text_color);
header("Content-Type: image/png");
imagepng($image);
imagedestroy($image);
?>
```

7.11   Image Creation from User Input

Image creation from user input in PHP refers to the process of dynamically generating an image based on parameters provided by the user, such as width, height, and other attributes. This technique allows users to customize the appearance of the image.

The process typically involves the following steps:

1. Collecting User Input: Collect data from the user using an HTML form.

2. Creating the Image: The imagecreate() function is used to create a blank image with the user-specified dimensions.

3. Adding Content to the Image: Additional content like text, shapes, or colors can be added to the image using functions like imagestring().

4. Outputting or Saving the Image: The final image is either displayed in the browser or saved to a file, typically in formats like PNG or JPEG.

This approach is useful in applications where images need to be generated on the fly, based on user preferences, such as in custom graphics, dynamic banners, or user-generated content.

```php
<?php
if (isset($_POST["n3"]))
{
    // Retrieve user input for width and height
    $a = $_POST["n1"];
    $b = $_POST["n2"];
    // Create an image with the specified width and height
    $image = imagecreate($a, $b);
    // Allocate a background color (white)
    $background_color = imagecolorallocate($image, 255, 255, 255);
    // Allocate a text color (blue)
    $text_color = imagecolorallocate($image, 0, 0, 255);
    // Add text to the image
    imagestring($image, 5, 180, 100, "reachandrises", $text_color);
    imagestring($image, 3, 160, 120, "A computer science portal",
    $text_color);
    // Set the content type header to PNG so the browser knows it's
an image
    header("Content-Type: image/png");
    // Output the image as a PNG
    imagepng($image);
    // Free up memory
    imagedestroy($image);
}
?>
```

Program: 7.11 Image Creation from User Input

```
first.php
<!DOCTYPE html>
<html lang="en">
<head>
    <meta charset="UTF-8">
      <meta name="viewport" content="width=device-width, initial-
scale=1.0">
    <title>Image Creator</title>
</head>
<body>
    <h1>Create a Custom Image</h1>
    <form action="second.php" method="post">
        <label for="n1">Width:</label>
        <input type="number" name="n1" id="n1" required>
        <br><br>
        <label for="n2">Height:</label>
        <input type="number" name="n2" id="n2" required>
        <br><br>
        <input type="submit" name="n3" value="Create Image">
    </form>
</body>
</html>
```

WORKING WITH FORMS

Introduction:

Forms in PHP are a fundamental part of web development, serving as the bridge between users and servers. They allow users to input data, which is then processed by a PHP script on the server side. Forms are typically composed of various input elements like text fields, checkboxes, radio buttons, dropdowns, and buttons, all wrapped in an HTML <form> tag.

In PHP, handling forms involves a few key steps: creating the form in HTML, submitting the form data, and processing that data using PHP. The data can be sent either via the HTTP GET or POST method, which determines how the form data is transmitted from the client to the server.

Handling form data in PHP involves more than just receiving the input; it requires proper validation to ensure that the data is correct, complete, and safe to process. Validation typically occurs in two stages: client-side and server-side. Client-side validation, done using JavaScript or HTML5 attributes, provides immediate feedback to users before they submit the form. However, since client-side validation can be bypassed, server-side validation in PHP is essential for security. PHP validation checks ensure that all required fields are filled out, the data is in the correct format (e.g., validating that an email address is properly structured), and that malicious input, such as cross-site scripting (XSS) attempts, is sanitized.

Real-World Applications of Forms in PHP

1. **User Registration and Login**: Forms for creating accounts and logging in allow users to access personalized features on websites.

2. **Contact Forms**: Businesses use these forms to collect inquiries or feedback from customers, facilitating communication.

3. **Surveys and Feedback**: Organizations gather user opinions and feedback through surveys to improve products and services.

4. **E-commerce Checkout**: Forms collect billing and shipping information during the checkout process for online purchases.

5. **Content Submission**: Websites that allow user-generated content use forms for submitting articles, comments, or reviews.

6. **Job Applications**: Companies have forms for candidates to submit their resumes and application details for job openings.

7. **Event Registration**: Forms enable users to register for events, workshops, and conferences, often including payment options.

8.1 Creating Forms:

User input is collected through an HTML form, which provides facilities for inputting text, numbers, values, emails, passwords, and control fields such as checkboxes, radio buttons, and submit buttons. Forms are commonly used to gather data from users. To create an HTML form, the <form> tag is used, which follows the syntax as,

```
<form>
    <!-- Form elements go here -->
</form>
```

8.1.1 <form> Elements:

In PHP, form elements are part of the HTML structure that allows users to input data, which is then processed by a PHP script. These elements include various input types like text fields, checkboxes, radio buttons, file inputs and more, each of which serves a specific purpose.

While PHP doesn't directly generate form elements (since they are part of HTML), it interacts with these elements by receiving and processing the data submitted by them.

One or more of the following form elements can be present in the HTML <form> elements:

- <input>
- <label>
- <select>

- <textarea>

- <input> **Element:**

The HTML <input> element is the most used form element. The <input> element in PHP is an HTML form element that allows users to provide data that can be processed by PHP on the server side. Although the <input> element itself is part of HTML, PHP interacts with the data submitted via this form element when handling form submissions.

An <input> element can be displayed in many ways as listed in table8.1, depending on the   type attribute.

Table. 8.1

Type	Description
<input type="text">	Displays a single-line text input field
<input type="radio">	Displays a radio button.
<input type="checkbox">	Displays a checkbox.
<input type="submit">	Displays a submit button.
<input type="button">	Displays a clickable button.

<Label>: The use of the <label> tag in HTML is intended to enhance usability for mouse users. i.e, if a user clicks on the text within the <label> element, it toggles the control. It is also useful for users with disabilities, especially those who use screen readers. When a label is properly associated with a form element, it helps screen readers understand and describe the form elements. The <label> tag defines the label for <button>, <input>, <select>, or <textarea> element etc.

The <label> tag can be used in two ways:

Firstly, use the <label> tag with a for attribute that matches the id attribute of the <input> element. This creates an explicit association between the label and the input, enhancing accessibility.The example code is shown below

```
<label for="username">Username:</label>
<input type="text" id="username" name="username">
```

Alternatively, you can place the <input> tag directly inside the <label> tag. In this case, the for and id attributes are not needed because the association is implicit. The example code is shown below

```
<label>Username:
    <input type="text" name="username">
</label>
```

for: The for attribute specifies which input control the label is associated with. Its value must match the id attribute of the corresponding <input> element.

<Select>: The <select> element creates a drop-down list with one or more options. It is highly customizable, and PHP interacts with it by processing the selected option(s) after the form is submitted. The <select> element contains one or more <option> elements, each representing an individual choice in the dropdown list.

The <option> element defines the choices available in the list. By default, the first item in the drop-down list is selected. To define a pre-selected option, add the selected attribute to the desired <option> element.

```
<select name="cars" >
<option >Volvo</option>
<option >Saab</option>
<option >Mercedes</option>
<option >Audi</option>
</select>
```

<textarea>: The <textarea> element defines a multi-line text input control. The <textarea> element is often used in a form, to collect user inputs like comments or reviews.

Rows and columns are two attributes that are mainly used in textarea tag.

rows: The rows attribute specifies the number of visible text lines for the textarea. This sets the height of the textarea.

Example:

```
rows="5"
```

cols: The cols attribute specifies the visible width (number of characters per line) of a text area. This sets the width of the textarea.

Example:

```
cols="30"
```

Syntax:

```
<textarea rows="5" cols="5">
    Multiple lines of text……..
</textarea>
Handling form elements in PHP is an essential aspect of building
dynamic, interactive web applications. Form elements such as
<input>,<label>, <select>, <textarea> and others are used to collect
user input, which PHP processes on the server side.
```

The usage of 'form elements' is shown in program 8.1.1

Program 8.1.1: Form Elements

```
<!DOCTYPE html>
<html>
<head>
    <title>Form Example</title>
</head>
<body>
    <form action="submit_form.php" method="post">
        <label for="username">Username:</label>
        <input type="text" id="username" name="username" required>
<br>
                <label for="password">Password:</label>
            <input type="password" id="password" name="password"
required>
<br>

                <label for="comments">Comments:</label>
        <textarea id="comments" name="comments" rows="4" cols="50"></
textarea>
                <br>
```

```
   <label>Gender:</label>
          <label><input type="radio" name="gender" value="male">
Male</label>
     <br>
  <label><input type="radio" name="gender" value="female"> Female</
label>
               <label for="country">Country:</label>
        <select id="country" name="country">
           <option value="usa">United States</option>
           <option value="canada">Canada</option>
           <option value="uk">United Kingdom</option>
        </select>
<br>

               <input type="submit" value="submit">
    </form>
</body>
</html>
```

8.1.2   Form Attributes:

When working with forms in PHP, the HTML form attributes play a vital role in defining the behavior, functionality, and appearance of the form and its elements. These attributes allow PHP to interact with the form data submitted by the user and process it on the server side.

The most important attributes for forms in PHP include,

Action:

Specifies the URL where the form data will be sent after submission. It can be .php, .jsp, .asp,.html etc. or any URL where you want to process your form. If the action attribute value is empty, action is set to the current page.

Example:

```
<form action="process.php">
```

If left empty (action=""), the form will submit to the current page.

Method:

This attribute defines the HTTP method used for form submission, either GET or POST.

- **GET:** The form values will be visible in the address bar of the new browser tab after submitting the form (GET is used for retrieving data through URL parameters).

- **POST:** In the post method, after the submission of the form, the form values will not be visible in the address bar of the new browser tab as they were before (POST is used for sensitive or large amounts of data).

Example:

```
<form method="POST">
```

Target: this attribute specifies where to display the response after the form is submitted, such as in a new tab or frame.

Example:

```
<form target="_blank"> to open the result in a new tab.
```

Value	Meaning
_blank	The link is displayed in a new window or tab.
_self	It is the default value. The link is displayed in the current window
_top	The link is displayed in the full body of the window

Basic structure of form attributes is shown below,

```
<form action="URL" method="post" target="_blank">
    <!-- Form elements go here -->
</form>
```

These attributes help define how the form interacts with the server, ensuring efficient data handling and controlling how the form behaves when submitted. Understanding these form attributes is essential for building secure, responsive, and user-friendly web forms in PHP-based applications.

Program 8.1.2: Form Attributes

```
<!DOCTYPE html>
<html>
<head>
<title>
HTML Forms
</title>
</head>
<body style="text-align:center;">
<h3> HTML Forms </h3>
<form action="home.php" method="GET" target="_blank">
<input type="submit" value="Submit">
</form>
</body>
</html>
home.php
<!DOCTYPE html>
<html>
<body>
<h2>Home Page</h2>
</body>
</html>
```

8.2   Accessing Form Input with User defined Arrays

Accessing form input in PHP using user-defined arrays allows you to organize and manage data more effectively, especially when dealing with multiple inputs or structured data. This can be particularly useful when creating complex forms where related fields need to be grouped together.

When a script receives data from a form, it typically gets a single value corresponding to each input name. However, you can modify this behavior by naming the input elements with an ending set of square brackets []. This technique allows the form to send multiple values for a single name and creating an array of values.

```
<select name="products[]" multiple>
    <option value="product1">Product 1</option>
    <option value="product2">Product 2</option>
    <option value="product3">Product 3</option>
    <option value="product4">Product 4</option>
</select>
```

Program: 8.2 Accessing Form Input with User defined Arrays:

```html
<html>
<head><title> An HTML form including a SELECT element</title></head>
<body>
<form action="process.php" method="post">
    <label for="colors">Choose your favorite colors:</label><br>
    <input type="checkbox" id="red" name="colors[]" value="red">
    <label for="red">Red</label><br>
  <input type="checkbox" id="green" name="colors[]" value="green">
    <label for="green">Green</label><br>
    <input type="checkbox" id="blue" name="colors[]" value="blue">
    <label for="blue">Blue</label><br>
    <input type="submit" value="Submit">
</form>
</body>
</html>
process.php
<?php
// Check if form data is received
if (isset($_POST['colors']) && is_array($_POST['colors']))
{
    // Retrieve the array of selected colors
    $colors = $_POST['colors'];

    // Display the selected colors
    echo "<h1>Selected Colors:</h1>";
    echo "<ul>";
    foreach ($colors as $color)
{
echo "<li>" . $color . "</li>";    }
    echo "</ul>";
} else
{
    echo "<p>No colors were selected.</p>";
}
?>
```

8.3   Combining HTML and PHP code on a single Page

Combining HTML and PHP code on a single page means embedding PHP code within an HTML file to dynamically generate HTML content based on server-side processing. This integration enables the web page to perform tasks such as form processing, data retrieval, and content customization while leveraging the HTML structure for presentation.

8.3.1   Embedding PHP in HTML:

PHP code can be directly included within an HTML file by using the <?php ?> tags. This allows for the generation of dynamic content.

Program 8.3.1: Embedding PHP in HTML

```html
<!DOCTYPE html>
<html>
<head>
    <title>My Page</title>
</head>
<body>
    <h1>Welcome!</h1>
    <p>Today's date is: <?php echo date('Y-m-d'); ?></p>
</body>
</html>
```

8.3.2   HTML Within PHP:

You can also write HTML code inside a PHP file, using echo or print statements.

Program 8.3.2: HTML Within PHP

```php
<?php
echo "<h1>" . "hello world" . "</h1>";
?>
```

8.3.3   Separate HTML and PHP Sections Combined by Using Form Method

Separate HTML and PHP Sections Combined by Using Form Method. A separate HTML form submits data to a PHP script. The PHP script processes the data and can return a result.

Program 8.3.3: Separate HTML and PHP Sections Combined by Using Form Method

```
<!-- form.html -->
<form action="process.php" method="post">
    <label for="name">Name:</label>
    <input type="text" id="name" name="name">
    <button type="submit">Submit</button>
</form>
<!-- process.php -->
<?php
if ($_SERVER["REQUEST_METHOD"] == "POST")
{
    $name = htmlspecialchars($_POST['name']);
    echo "<h1>Hello, $name!</h1>";
}
?>
```

8.3.4 Using include statement:

Using the include statement in PHP allows you to separate code into multiple files and include them into a single script. This approach is useful for maintaining modular code, reusing components, and keeping your codebase organized.

Program 8.3.4: Embedded PHP in HTML Using the include Statement:

```
first.php
<!DOCTYPE html>
<html lang="en">
<head>
    <title>My Website</title>
</head>
<body>
        <h1>Welcome to My Website</h1>
<?php include 'first.php'; ?>
</body>
</html>
footer.php
    <footer>
        <p>&copy; 2024 My Website</p>
    </footer>
```

These methods provide flexibility in combining HTML and PHP, allowing for dynamic content generation and better code organization.

8.4   Using Hidden Fields to save state

Hidden fields are a type of input field in HTML forms that are not visible to the user but can store data that should be submitted with the form. They allow developers to maintain state information across different page requests without displaying this data to the user.

8.4.1   Purpose of Hidden Fields:

- **State Management:** Hidden fields are used to retain information that needs to persist across form submissions. For instance, you may want to remember user selections, session IDs, or other data without displaying it on the page.

- **Data Transfer:** They can carry information from one page to another without requiring the user to input it each time.

8.4.2   How Hidden Fields Work:

Hidden fields are defined in an HTML form using the <input> tag with the type set to "hidden."

When the form is submitted, the values of these hidden fields are sent along with the visible form data, making them accessible to the server-side code (e.g., PHP code).

Program 8.4: Using Hidden Fields to save state

```
<html>
<body>
<form method="post" action="first.php">
    <input type="text" name="userInput">
    <input type="hidden" name="sessionId" value="12345">
    <input type="submit" value="Submit">
</form>
</body>
</html>
```

In this example:

- userInput is a visible text field where users can input data.

- sessionId is a hidden field that contains a value (e.g., a session identifier).

You can access the data from the hidden fields after form submission using the following PHP program

```
first.php
<?php
if ($_SERVER["REQUEST_METHOD"] == "POST")
{
    $userInput = $_POST["userInput"];
    $sessionId = $_POST["sessionId"];
    echo "User Input: " .$userInput . "<br>";
    echo "Session ID: " . $sessionId;
}?>
```

8.5   Redirecting the user

Redirection from one page to another in PHP is commonly achieved using header function.

8.5.1   Using Header Function in PHP:

The header() function is an inbuilt function in PHP which is used to redirecting from one page to another .

Basic Redirection:

```
header('Location: http://www.example.com/');
exit; // Important to terminate the script after redirection.
```

Redirection with HTTP Status Codes: You can specify an HTTP status code to indicate whether the redirection is temporary or permanent:

```
header('Location: http://www.example.com/', true, 301); // Permanent
redirect
exit;
```

Parameters: This function accepts three parameters as mentioned above and described below:

1. **Location:** This indicates the URL to which the user should be redirected.

2. **true:** This indicates that the header should replace any previous Location header. It ensures that only the most recent redirect is applied.

3. **Status code:** This specifies the HTTP response code for a permanent redirect or temporary redirect.

- **Temporary Redirect (302):** Use when the move is not permanent and the original URL will be back.

- **Permanent Redirect (301):** Use when the move is permanent and you want search engines to update their records.

Program 8.5: Redirecting the user

```php
<?php
// Redirect to the thank you page
header('Location: thank_you.php', true, 301);
exit; // Stop further execution
?>
thank_you.php:
<html>
<head>
    <meta charset="UTF-8">
    <title>Thank You</title>
</head>
<body>
    <h1>Thank You!</h1>
    <p>Your submission has been received.</p>
</body>
</html>
```

8.6 Sending Mail on Form Submission

The PHP mail() function is a built-in function that enables developers to send emails directly from their applications. The syntax for the mail() function is as follows:

```php
mail("$to", $subject, $message, $headers);
```

Parameters of the mail() Function:

1. **$to**: This parameter contains the recipient's email address, where the email will be sent.

2. **$subject**: This parameter represents the subject line of the email.

3. **$message**: This parameter holds the content of the email, which can include text, HTML, or other formats.

4. **$headers**: This optional parameter is used to specify additional headers, such as Cc (carbon copy) and Bcc (blind carbon copy).

Sending Emails Using HTML Forms:

To send an email using an HTML form, the form's action attribute should point to a PHP script that handles the submission. The script will utilize the mail() function to process the data from the form.

Program 8.6: Sending Emails Using HTML Forms
HTML Form (form.php)

The following code presents a simple contact form that collects the user's email and message.

```html
<!DOCTYPE html>
<html lang="en">
<head>
    <meta charset="UTF-8">
    <title>Contact Form</title>
</head>
<body>
    <h1>Contact Us</h1>
    <form action="send_mail.php" method="POST">
        <label for="email">Your Email:</label>
        <input type="email" id="email" name="email" required>
            <label for="message">Message:</label>
        <textarea id="message" name="message" required></textarea>
            <input type="submit" value="Send">
    </form>
</body>
</html>
```

PHP Script to Handle Mail Sending (send_mail.php)

The following PHP script processes the form submission and sends the email using the mail() function.

```php
<?php
if ($_SERVER["REQUEST_METHOD"] == "POST")
{
    // Retrieve form data
    $to = "scim@gmail.com"; // Recipient's email address
    $subject = "PHP Form Submission"; // Subject of the email
  $message = htmlspecialchars($_POST['message']); // User's message
    $headers = "From: " . htmlspecialchars($_POST['email']); //
Sender's email


    // Send the email
    if (mail($to, $subject, $message, $headers))
{

        echo "Email sent successfully!";
    } else
{

        echo "Failed to send email.";
    }}?>
```

How It Works

1. **User Interaction:** The user accesses form.php, fills out the contact form, and submits it.

2. **Form Submission:** The data is sent to send_mail.php via the POST method.

3. **Email Processing:** The send_mail.php script retrieves the user's email and message, sanitizes the input to prevent injection attacks, and uses the mail() function to send the email.

4. **Confirmation Message:** After processing, the script provides feedback to the user, indicating whether the email was successfully sent.

Note: The mail() function in PHP works effectively in online environments where the server is configured to send emails. This typically involves using built-in SMTP settings provided by web hosting services, allowing for seamless email delivery from the application.

INTERACTING WITH MYSQL USING PHP

Introduction

In modern web development, most dynamic websites and applications rely on databases to store, retrieve, and manage data. Whether it's user information, product catalogs, or blog content, databases are the backbone of many web applications. PHP, as one of the most popular server-side scripting languages, provides extensive support for interacting with databases, enabling developers to create powerful, data-driven websites.

Why Databases?

Data is the heart of any application, and managing it efficiently is crucial. A database allows you to store large amounts of structured information and quickly retrieve, update, or delete data as needed. By using databases, your PHP applications can:

- **Store Persistent Data**: Unlike session data or variables, which are temporary, databases store information that persists across user sessions.

- **Handle Large Datasets**: Databases are optimized for searching, sorting, and managing large volumes of data efficiently.

- **Organize Information**: Using tables and relationships, databases can manage complex data in a logical and scalable way.

- **Enable Multi-user Access**: Databases are designed to handle concurrent requests from multiple users, making them essential for scalable applications.

PHP and Databases

PHP has built-in functions and extensions that allow seamless interaction with various database systems, such as MySQL, PostgreSQL, and SQLite. The most common combination is PHP with MySQL, thanks to the LAMP stack (Linux, Apache, MySQL, PHP), which has become a standard in web development.

PHP supports databases through:

- **MySQLi (MySQL Improved Extension)**: An extension specifically designed for MySQL databases, offering both procedural and object-oriented interfaces.

- **PDO (PHP Data Objects)**: A database abstraction layer that provides a uniform interface for interacting with multiple types of databases, such as MySQL, PostgreSQL, and SQLite.

Real-world Applications

Understanding databases is essential because they are used in almost every web application:

- **E-commerce platforms**: Store and manage product data, orders, and customer information.

- **Content Management Systems (CMS)**: Like WordPress, which rely heavily on databases to manage articles, pages, and users.

- **Social Networks**: Manage user profiles, posts, comments, and interactions.

- **Online Forms and User Authentication**: Store user-submitted data and manage login credentials.

9.1   MySQL Versus MySQLi Functions

MySQL: A widely used relational database management system (RDBMS) that utilizes SQL (Structured Query Language) for database operations.

MySQLi (MySQL Improved): An enhanced extension of MySQL designed for PHP, offering improved functionality and security features.Planning and Creating Database Tables.

Comparison between MySQL Versus MySQLi:

Features	MySQL Functions	MySQLi Functions
Programming Style	Procedural only	Supports both procedural and OOP
Security	No support for prepared statements	Supports prepared statements
Transaction Support	No	Yes
Advanced Features	Limited	Includes transactions, error handling
Function Examples	mysql_connect(), mysql_query()	mysqli_connect(), mysqli_query()

MySQL Functions

- **Deprecated Status**: As of PHP 5.5.0, the MySQL extension is deprecated and removed in PHP 7.0.0.

- **Procedural Interface**: The MySQL extension only allows a procedural programming style, which may limit coding flexibility.

- **Function Examples:**

  - mysql_connect(): Opens a connection to the MySQL server.

  - mysql_query(): Executes a query against the database.

  - mysql_fetch_array(): Fetches a result row as an associative or numeric array.

MySQLi Functions

- **Improved Interface**: MySQLi offers an enhanced interface for interacting with MySQL databases.

- **Flexibility**: Supports both procedural and object-oriented programming styles, catering to different developer preferences.

- **Security Features**: Prepared statements mitigate SQL injection risks, making applications more secure.

- **Function Examples:**

  - **Procedural:**

    - mysqli_connect(): Opens a connection to the MySQL server.

    - mysqli_query(): Executes a query against the database.

    - mysqli_fetch_array(): Fetches a result row as an associative or numeric array.

  - **Object-Oriented:**

    - $mysqli = new mysqli(...): Creates a new MySQLi connection instance.

    - $mysqli->query(...): Executes a query on the established connection.

    - $result->fetch_array(): Retrieves a row from the result set.

9.2 Database Table Management: Creation, Insertion, and Deletion Operations

9.2.1 Creating Database Tables

Creating database tables is a crucial step in designing a relational database. This process involves defining the structure of the table, including its columns, data types, and any constraints that ensure data integrity.

SQL Command for Table Creation

The basic syntax for creating a table in SQL is as follows:

```
CREATE TABLE table_name (
    column1 datatype [constraints],
    column2 datatype [constraints],
    column3 datatype [constraints],
    ...
);
```

- **table_name**: The name of the table being created.
- **column1, column2, column3, ...**: The names of the columns in the table.
- **data_type**: The type of data that each column will hold (e.g., INT, VARCHAR, DATE).
- **constraints**: Optional rules that define the properties of the column (e.g., PRIMARY KEY, NOT NULL, UNIQUE).

Example for the Student Table

To create a Students table that holds student information, the following SQL command can be used:

```
CREATE TABLE student (
    name VARCHAR(50),
    phonenumber VARCHAR(15),
    email VARCHAR(100),
    address VARCHAR(100)
);
```

9.2.2   Inserting Data into Tables:

In SQL, inserting data into tables is a fundamental operation that adds new records to a database. The primary command for this operation is the INSERT INTO statement. This command can insert either a single row of data or multiple rows at once.

SQL Command for Data Insertion

The basic syntax for the INSERT INTO command is as follows:

```
INSERT INTO table_name (column1, column2, column3, ...)
VALUES (value1, value2, value3, ...);
```

- **table_name**: The name of the table where data will be inserted.
- **column1, column2, column3, ...**: The columns in the table to populate. You can list all the columns or only the specific ones needed.
- **value1, value2, value3, ...**: The corresponding values for each specified column.

Example

Consider a simple example with a table named Students, which has the following columns: id, name, and age. To insert a single record into the Students table, use the following SQL command:

```
INSERT INTO student (name, phonenumber, email, address)  VALUES
('ravi', '88xxxx, 'ravi@gmail.com', 'india');
```

Multiple rows can be inserted using the following syntax:

```
INSERT INTO table_name (column1, column2, column3, ...)
VALUES
    (value1a, value2a, value3a),
    (value1b, value2b, value3b),
    (value1c, value2c, value3c);
```

9.2.3   Managing Data in Tables

i. Deleting Data

Managing data in tables involves operations that allow for modifying, deleting, and restructuring the data stored within a database. Here are three key operations: deleting data, truncating data, and dropping a table.

i. Deleting Data

To remove all records from the table while keeping the table structure intact, use the following SQL command:

Syntax:

```
DELETE FROM student;
```

This command will delete all rows in the Students table. However, it can be filtered with a WHERE clause to remove specific records. For example:

```
DELETE FROM Students WHERE id = 1;
```

ii. Truncating Data

To quickly remove all records from the table while keeping the table structure intact:

Syntax:

```
TRUNCATE TABLE student;
```

Key Differences from DELETE:

- TRUNCATE is faster than DELETE as it does not log individual row deletions.
- It resets any auto-incrementing columns to their starting values.
- TRUNCATE cannot be rolled back if the table is not in a transaction.

iii. Dropping the Table

To remove the table entirely from the database, including its structure and all associated data, use:

Syntax:

```
DROP TABLE student;
```

This command permanently deletes the Students table and cannot be undone. All data and the table schema will be lost.

These operations are essential for managing data effectively within a database environment.

9.3   Connecting to MySQL with PHP

Connecting to a MySQL database using PHP involves a series of steps to ensure that the connection is established correctly. Below are the steps required to set up a connection using the MySQLi extension.

Step 1: Set Up Connection Variables:

This step involves defining the parameters required to connect to MySQL database. The connection variables are:

- **Server Name:** This is usually localhost if database is hosted on the same server as PHP script.
- **Username:** The username for accessing the database, commonly root for local setups.
- **Password:** The password associated with the database user, which may be empty for local installations.

Defining connection parameters:

```php
$servername = "localhost";   // Server name
$username = "root";          // Database username
$password = "";              // Database password
```

Step 2: Create the Connection: Use the MySQLi extension to establish a connection.

```php
$conn = new mysqli($servername, $username, $password);
```

Step 3: Check the Connection
It's important to verify that the connection was successful. Use the following code for checking the connection

```php
if ($conn->connect_error)
{
    die("Connection failed: " . $conn->connect_error);
}
echo "Connected successfully";
```

If the connection fails, an error message will be displayed, terminating the script. If successful, a confirmation message will be shown.

Step 4: Close the Connection
Although the connection will close automatically at the end of the script, it's good practice to close it manually for better resource management:

```php
$conn->close(); // Close the connection
```

This process allows PHP scripts to interact with MySQL databases effectively, enabling data retrieval and manipulation.

Program 9.3: Connecting to MySQL with PHP:

```php
<?php
// Step 1: Set Up Your Connection Variables
$servername = "localhost"; // The name of the server hosting the
database
$username = "root";          // The username for database access
$password = "";              // The password for the database user


// Step 2: Create the Connection
$conn = new mysqli($servername, $username, $password);
// Step 3: Check the Connection
if ($conn->connect_error)
{
    die("Connection failed: " . $conn->connect_error);
}
echo "Connected successfully";
// Step 4: Close the Connection
$conn->close(); // Close the connection
?>
```

9.4   Working with MySQL Data

Working with MySQL Data refers to the various operations performed on data stored in a MySQL database using SQL (Structured Query Language). These operations typically include:

- **Creating Table:** To define a new table and its structure, use the CREATE TABLE statement.

- **Inserting Data**: Adding new records to a database table. To add data to a table, use the INSERT statement.

- **Retrieving Data**: Querying the database to access and display existing records. To fetch data from a table, use the SELECT statement.

- **Updating Data**: Modifying existing records in the database: To modify existing records, use the UPDATE statement.

- **Deleting Data**: Removing records from the database. To remove records, use the DELETE statement. .

9.5 Table Creation in MySQL using PHP

To create a table in MySQL using PHP, follow these steps.

Step 1: Set Up Database Connection

It defines the necessary parameters such as the server name, username, password, and database name. Upon executing the connection, it checks for any connection errors. If an error occurs, the script will terminate and display an error message. This setup is crucial for interacting with the database, allowing for further operations like querying and modifying data within the specified database.

```php
<?php
// Step 1: Set Up Your Connection Variables
$servername = "localhost"; // The name of the server hosting the
database
$username = "root";        // The username for database access
$password = "";            // The password for the database user
$dbname = "rayna";         // The name of the database
// Create connection
$conn = new mysqli($servername, $username, $password, $dbname);
if ($conn->connect_error)
{
    die("Connection failed: " . $conn->connect_error);
}
?>
```

Step 2: Create the SQL Query to Create a Table

Next, write the SQL statement to create a table. For example, a student table with fields for id, name, email, phonenumber and address can be created:

```php
$sql = "CREATE TABLE student (
    id INT(11) AUTO_INCREMENT PRIMARY KEY,
    name VARCHAR(50) NOT NULL,
    phonenumber VARCHAR(15) NOT NULL,
    email VARCHAR(100) NOT NULL,
    address VARCHAR(255) NOT NULL
)";
```

This SQL statement defines the structure of the student table, where id serves as a unique identifier for each student and automatically increments with each new entry. The name, phonenumber, email, and address fields are set as mandatory (NOT NULL), ensuring that essential information is always captured. Using appropriate data types, such as VARCHAR for text fields, ensures efficient storage and retrieval of student information.

Step 3: Execute the Query

Now, execute the query to create the table:

```php
if ($conn->query($sql) = = = TRUE)
{
    echo "Table 'student' created successfully";
} else
{
    echo "Error creating table: " . $conn->error;
}
```

If the table is created successfully, a success message is displayed, confirming the creation of the student table. If an error occurs during execution, an error message is shown, providing details about the issue, which helps in debugging and maintaining the database structure.

Step 4: Close the Connection

Finally, close the connection to the database:

```php
$conn->close();
```

Program 9.5: Table Creation in MySQL using PHP

```php
<?php
// Step 1: Set Up Your Connection Variables
$servername = "localhost"; // The name of the server hosting the
database
$username = "root";        // The username for database access
$password = "";            // The password for the database user
$dbname = "rayna";         // The name of the database
// Create connection
$conn = new mysqli($servername, $username, $password, $dbname);
if ($conn->connect_error)
{
    die("Connection failed: " . $conn->connect_error);
}
// Step 2: Write the SQL Query to Create the Table
$sql = "CREATE TABLE student (
    id INT(11) AUTO_INCREMENT PRIMARY KEY,
    name VARCHAR(50) NOT NULL,
    phonenumber VARCHAR(15) NOT NULL,
    email VARCHAR(100) NOT NULL,
    address VARCHAR(255) NOT NULL
)";
// step:3 Execute the query
if ($conn->query($sql) === TRUE)
{
    echo "Table 'student' created successfully";
} else
{
    echo "Error creating table: " . $conn->error;
}


//step:4 Close the connection
$conn->close();
?>
```

9.6   Using PHP to Insert Data into a Database

This section covers the process of inserting data into a database table using PHP. It involves creating an HTML form to collect user input, such as name, email, phone number, and address. Upon submission, the form data is sent to a PHP script, which processes the input and executes an SQL INSERT statement to add the data to the specified database table. This approach allows for efficient data entry and management within web applications, facilitating interaction between users and the database. Proper handling of user input and error checking are crucial for maintaining data integrity and security.

To insert data into a database table using a form in PHP, follow these steps:

Step 1: Create an HTML Form:

Create an HTML Form: This form will collect user input, such as name and email. The form will submit data to a PHP script for processing.Here's an example of an HTML form to collect user data:

```
index.php:
<!DOCTYPE html>
<html lang="en">
<head>
    <meta charset="UTF-8">
      <meta name="viewport" content="width=device-width, initial-
scale=1.0">
    <title>Insert Student Data</title>
</head>
<body>
    <h1>Student Registration Form</h1>
    <form action="insert.php" method="post">
        <label for="name">Name:</label>
        <input type="text" id="name" name="name" required><br><br>

        <label for="phonenumber">Phone Number:</label>
          <input type="number" id="phonenumber" name="phonenumber"
required><br><br>

        <label for="email">Email:</label>
      <input type="email" id="email" name="email" required><br><br>

        <label for="address">Address:</label>
      <input type="text" id="address" name="address" required><br><br>

        <input type="submit" value="Submit">
    </form>
</body>
</html>
```

This form includes input fields for all necessary data, ensuring that users provide complete information. The required attribute enforces that each field must be filled out before submission, enhancing data integrity. When the form is submitted, it sends the data to the specified PHP script (insert.php) for processing, enabling seamless interaction between the user interface and the backend database.

Step 2: Handle the Input with PHP

Create a PHP file (e.g., insert.php) to handle the form submission and insert the data into the database. This script will process the incoming data from the HTML form, establish a connection to the database, and execute an SQL INSERT statement to store the submitted information.

Here's a basic outline of how the insert.php file can be structured:

```php
<?php
$servername = "localhost";
$username = "root";
$password = "";
$dbname = "rayna";

// Create connection
$conn = new mysqli($servername, $username, $password, $dbname);

// Check connection
if ($conn->connect_error)
{
    die("Connection failed: " . $conn->connect_error);
}
$name = $_POST['name'];
$phonenumber = $_POST['phonenumber'];
$email = $_POST['email'];
$address = $_POST['address'];

// Assuming $sql is defined earlier
$sql = "INSERT INTO student (name, phonenumber, email, address)
VALUES ('$name', '$phonenumber', '$email', '$address')";
```

```php
// Execute the query
$result = mysqli_query($conn, $sql);


if ($result)
{
    echo "Record inserted successfully";
} else
{
    echo "Error inserting record: " . mysqli_error($conn);
}
// Step 7: Close the connection
$conn->close();

?>
```

9.7 Using PHP to Retrieve Data:

This section focuses on the process of retrieving data from a MySQL database using PHP. It involves querying the database to access and display existing records, typically utilizing the SELECT statement. The process begins by establishing a connection to the database with appropriate credentials, ensuring a secure and successful connection.

Next, a SQL query is executed to fetch the desired records from a specified table. After retrieving the data, it is formatted and displayed on a webpage using HTML.

Steps to Retrieve Data from a MySQL Database

1. **Establish a Database Connection**: Create a PHP file that connects to the MySQL database using the appropriate credentials (server name, username, password, and database name).

2. **Execute a SQL Query**: Use the SELECT statement to query the database and retrieve the desired records from a specified table.

3. **Display the Results**: Format and display the retrieved data on a webpage using HTML, ensuring to sanitize the output for security.

Program 9.7: Create a PHP File to Retrieve Data

Create a PHP file (e.g., retrieve.php) that will connect to the database and retrieve the student records.

```php
<?php
$servername = "localhost";
$username = "root";
$password = "";
$dbname = "rayna";

// Create connection
$conn = new mysqli($servername, $username, $password, $dbname);

// Check connection
if ($conn->connect_error)
{
    die("Connection failed: " . $conn->connect_error);
}
// Query to select data
$query = "SELECT name, phonenumber, email, address FROM student";
$s = mysqli_query($conn, $query);
// Start HTML output
?>
<!DOCTYPE html>
<html lang="en">
<head>
    <meta charset="UTF-8">
      <meta name="viewport" content="width=device-width, initial-scale=1.0">
    <title>Address Book View</title>
</head>
<body>
<table border="1">
    <tr>
        <th>Name</th>
        <th>Phone Number</th>
        <th>Email</th>
        <th>Address</th>
    </tr>
```

```php
<?php
while ($result = $s->fetch_assoc())
{
    ?>
    <tr>
        <td><?php echo htmlspecialchars($result['name']); ?></td>
            <td><?php echo htmlspecialchars($result['phonenumber']);
?></td>
        <td><?php echo htmlspecialchars($result['email']); ?></td>
      <td><?php echo htmlspecialchars($result['address']); ?></td>
    </tr>
    <?php
}
?>
</table>
<?php
// Close the connection
$conn->close();
?>
</body>
</html>
```

9.8   Using PHP to Update Data

This section focuses on the process of updating existing records in a MySQL database using PHP. It involves creating a user interface that allows users to modify previously entered data. The process begins with establishing a connection to the database using the necessary credentials, ensuring secure access.

Next, an HTML form is created to collect updated information from users, including fields for the data to be modified and a unique identifier to specify which record to update. Upon form submission, a PHP script processes the input, prepares an SQL UPDATE statement, and executes it to make the necessary changes in the database.

This functionality is crucial for maintaining accurate and current data in web applications, allowing users to easily correct or update information as needed. Proper validation and error handling are essential to ensure data integrity and security throughout the update process.

Modifying existing records in the database: To modify existing records, use the UPDATE statement.

To update data in a MySQL database using PHP, follow these steps:

1. **Fetch the data from the database** and display it in an HTML table.
2. **Create an update form** that is populated with the selected record's data.
3. **Process the form submission** to update the database with the new information.

Step1: **Fetch the data from the database** and display it in an HTML table. This code connects to the database, retrieves data, and displays it in a table format.

```php
students.php
<?php
// Database credentials
$servername = "localhost";
$username = "root";
$password = "";
$dbname = "rayna";
// Create connection
$conn = new mysqli($servername, $username, $password, $dbname);
// Check connection
if ($conn->connect_error)
{
    die("Connection failed: " . $conn->connect_error);
}
```

```php
// Fetch students from the database
$sql = "SELECT id, name, phonenumber, email, address FROM students";
$result = $conn->query($sql);
?>
<!DOCTYPE html>
<html lang="en">
<head>
    <meta charset="UTF-8">
      <meta name="viewport" content="width=device-width, initial-scale=1.0">
    <title>Student List</title>
</head>
```

```php
<body>
    <h1>Student List</h1>
    <table border="1">
        <tr>
            <th>ID</th>
            <th>Name</th>
            <th>Phone Number</th>
            <th>Email</th>
            <th>Address</th>
            <th>Action</th>
        </tr>
        <?php
        if ($result->num_rows > 0)
{
            while ($row = $result->fetch_assoc())
{
                echo "<tr>
                    <td>{$row['id']}</td>
                    <td>{$row['name']}</td>
                    <td>{$row['phonenumber']}</td>
                    <td>{$row['email']}</td>
                    <td>{$row['address']}</td>
                    <td>
                    <form action='update_student.php' method='POST'>
                <input type='hidden' name='id' value='{$row['id']}'>
                            <input type='submit' value='Update'>
                        </form>
                    </td>
                </tr>";
            }
        } else
{
            echo "<tr><td colspan='6'>No students found</td></tr>";
        }
        ?>
    </table>
<?php
// Close connection
$conn->close();
?>
</body>
</html>
```

Step 2: Create an Update Form

This code retrieves the selected student's data and displays it in a form for updating.

```php
update_student.php
<?php
// Database credentials
$servername = "localhost";
$username = "root";
$password = "";
$dbname = "rayna";

// Create connection
$conn = new mysqli($servername, $username, $password, $dbname);

// Check connection
if ($conn->connect_error)
{
    die("Connection failed: " . $conn->connect_error);
}

// Check if an ID is provided
if (isset($_POST['id']))
{
    $id = $_POST['id'];
    // Fetch the student data
    $sql = "SELECT id, name, phonenumber, email, address FROM student WHERE id = ?";
    $stmt = $conn->prepare($sql);
    $stmt->bind_param("i", $id);
    $stmt->execute();
    $result = $stmt->get_result();
    $student = $result->fetch_assoc();
}
?>
```

```php
<!DOCTYPE html>
<html lang="en">
<head>
    <meta charset="UTF-8">
      <meta name="viewport" content="width=device-width, initial-scale=1.0">
    <title>Update Student</title>
</head>
<body>
    <h1>Update Student Information</h1>
    <form action="process_update.php" method="POST">
     <input type="hidden" name="id" value="<?php echo $student['id']; ?>">
        <label for="name">Name:</label>
        <input type="text" id="name" name="name" value="<?php echo $student['name']; ?>" required>
        <br>
        <label for="phonenumber">Phone Number:</label>
          <input type="text" id="phonenumber" name="phonenumber" value="<?php echo $student['phonenumber']; ?>" required>
        <br>
        <label for="email">Email:</label>
          <input type="email" id="email" name="email" value="<?php echo $student['email']; ?>" required>
        <br>
        <label for="address">Address:</label>
         <textarea id="address" name="address" required><?php echo $student['address']; ?></textarea>
        <br>
        <input type="submit" value="Update">
    </form>
<?php
// Close connection
$conn->close();
?>
</body>
</html>
```

Step 3: Process the Update

This code processes the form submission and updates the table record in the database.

process_update.php

```php
<?php
// Database credentials
$servername = "localhost";
$username = "root";
$password = "";
$dbname = "rayna";

// Create connection
$conn = new mysqli($servername, $username, $password, $dbname);

// Check connection
if ($conn->connect_error)
{
    die("Connection failed: " . $conn->connect_error);
}
// Check if the form is submitted
if ($_SERVER["REQUEST_METHOD"] == "POST")
{
    $id = $_POST['id'];
    $name = $_POST['name'];
    $phonenumber = $_POST['phonenumber'];
    $email = $_POST['email'];
    $address = $_POST['address'];
    // Prepare an update statement
    $sql = "UPDATE student SET name = ?, phonenumber = ?, email =
?, address = ? WHERE id = ?";
    $stmt = $conn->prepare($sql);

    if ($stmt)
{
        // Bind parameters
        $stmt->bind_param("ssssi", $name, $phonenumber, $email,
$address, $id);
```

```php
        // Execute the statement
        if ($stmt->execute())
{
            echo "Record updated successfully. <a href='students.
php'>Go back to the list</a>";
        } else
{
            echo "Error updating record: " . $stmt->error;
        }
        // Close statement
        $stmt->close();
    } else
{
        echo "Error preparing statement: " . $conn->error;
    }
}
// Close connection
$conn->close();
?>
```

9.9   Deleting Data in MySQL with PHP

Deletion mechanism can be accomplished in three ways:

9.9.1   Delete the Record Using the DELETE Command:

The DELETE command is used to remove specific records from a table based on a condition.This method allows for selective deletion of records.

```sql
DELETE FROM table_name WHERE condition;
```

Program 9.9.1 : Delete the Record Using the DELETE Command:

```php
<?php
// Step 1: Set Up Your Connection Variables
$servername = "localhost"; // Server name
$username = "root";        // Database username
$password = "";            // Database password
$dbname = "rayna";         // Database name

// Step 2: Create connection
$conn = new mysqli($servername, $username, $password, $dbname);

// Step 3: Check connection
if ($conn->connect_error)
{
    die("Connection failed: " . $conn->connect_error);
}

// Step 4: Define the ID of the record to delete

// Step 5: SQL Query to Delete the Record
$sql = "DELETE FROM student WHERE id = 10"; // Adjust table name and
condition as necessary

// Step 6: Execute the query
$result = mysqli_query($conn, $sql);
if ($result)
{
    echo «Record deleted successfully»;
} else
{
    echo "Error deleting record: " . mysqli_error($conn);
}

// Step 7: Close the connection
$conn->close();
?>
```

9.9.2 Truncating a Table Using the TRUNCATE Command:

The TRUNCATE command removes all rows from a table while keeping the table structure intact. This method is faster than using the DELETE command because it does not generate individual row delete logs. However, it cannot be rolled back, meaning that once the TRUNCATE command is executed, the action is permanent and cannot be undone.

Program 9.9.2: Truncating a Table Using the TRUNCATE Command

```php
<?php
// Step 1: Set Up Your Connection Variables
$servername = "localhost"; // Server name
$username = "root";        // Database username
$password = "";            // Database password
$dbname = "rayna";         // Database name

// Step 2: Create connection
$conn = new mysqli($servername, $username, $password, $dbname);

// Step 3: Check connection
if ($conn->connect_error)
{
    die("Connection failed: " . $conn->connect_error);
}

// Step 4: SQL Query to Truncate the Table
$sql = "TRUNCATE TABLE student"; // Adjust table name as necessary

// Step 5: Execute the query
$result = mysqli_query($conn, $sql);
if ($result)
{
    echo «All records deleted successfully from the <student>
table»;
} else
{
    echo "Error truncating table: " . mysqli_error($conn);
}

// Step 6: Close the connection
$conn->close();
?>
```

9.9.3   Dropping a Table in MySQL

Dropping a table means permanently removing it and all of its data from the database. This action cannot be undone, so it's important to be certain before executing the command.

Syntax:

The basic syntax for dropping a table is as follows:

```
DROP TABLE table_name;
```

Program 9.9.3: Dropping a Table in MySQL

```php
<?php
// Step 1: Set Up Your Connection Variables
$servername = "localhost"; // Server name
$username = "root";        // Database username
$password = "";            // Database password
$dbname = "rayna";         // Database name
// Create connection
$conn = new mysqli($servername, $username, $password, $dbname);
// Step 2: Check the Connection
if ($conn->connect_error)
{
    die("Connection failed: " . $conn->connect_error);
}
// Step 3: Write the SQL Query to Drop the Table
$sql = "DROP TABLE IF EXISTS student"; // Drop the 'student' table
if it exists
// Step 4: Execute the Query
if ($conn->query($sql) === TRUE)
{
    echo "Table 'student' dropped successfully";
} else
{
    echo "Error dropping table: " . $conn->error;
}
// Step 5: Close the Connection
$conn->close(); ?>
```

9.9.4   Difference Between Deleting and Truncating a Table

i. Deleting a Table

```
Command: DROP TABLE table_name;
```

- **Purpose**: Permanently removes the table and its structure from the database.
- **Data**: All data stored in the table is lost.
- **Use Case**: When you no longer need the table and want to completely remove it from the database.
- **Rollback**: This action cannot be undone without a backup.

Example:

```
$sql = "DROP TABLE IF EXISTS student";
```

ii. Truncating a Table

```
Command: TRUNCATE TABLE table_name;
```

- **Purpose**: Removes all rows from the table but keeps the table structure intact.
- **Data**: All data is deleted, but the table itself remains available for future use.
- **Use Case**: When you want to delete all records from the table quickly without affecting the table structure.
- **Rollback**: This action cannot be rolled back if not part of a transaction.

Example:

```
$sql = "TRUNCATE TABLE student";
```